Trust &
Tragedy

OTHER BOOKS BY TOMMY TENNEY

Bestselling Series
The God Chasers
God's Favorite House
The God Catchers

Unity Trilogy
God's Dream Team
Answering God's Prayer
God's Secret to Greatness

Additional Great Resources by Tommy Tenney
The God Catchers Workbook
Experiencing His Presence (Devotional)
Chasing God, Serving Man
How to be a God Chaser and a Kid Chaser
Secret Sources of Power
Extreme God Chasers (for youth)
The Daily Chase (Devotional)
The Heart of a God Chaser

Trust &
Tragedy

Encountering God in Times of Crisis

TOMMY TENNEY

THOMAS NELSON PUBLISHERS®
Nashville

A Division of Thomas Nelson, Inc.
www.ThomasNelson.com

CONTENTS

CHAPTER 1

TRAGEDY AND TOWERS
(Contemporary Crisis—Ancient Response)

Tragedy. Death. Sorrow. Pain.

The grim reality lurking behind these words has made the strongest men cry and has forced entire nations to their knees.

Each day thousands face personal tragedy and sorrow. Loved ones slip away into eternity and medical reports deliver the frightening prognoses we hoped we'd never hear. Marriages wither and die and layoff notices blanket a production floor, snuffing out countless personal dreams of security and "a better life."

The common sorrows of life often seem impossible to carry. None of us were prepared when tragedy violently changed the course of human history and established September 11 as humanity's new date "that will live in infamy."

We watched in disbelief while office workers in bloodied dresses and torn business suits fled from the burning World Trade Center towers in wide-eyed panic. We saw the images lurch and sway on our television screens as news camera operators were urged to run for their lives by anxious New York police officers and firefighters fitted in masks and oxygen tanks.

Viewers around the world heard the screams from New York's streets and watched live television images of New York's twin towers collapsing one after another in flames and smoke. Tragedy never seemed nearer as the bright morning sun disappeared behind the gloom of a choking cloud of ash. When the dust finally cleared enough for us to grasp what had happened, all we found was a twisted pile of steel and concrete measuring five stories high.

It didn't matter that the scene replayed before our eyes over and over again courtesy of the wonder of modern digital technology. Neither did it matter that the scene was beamed from one of the world's most cosmopolitan centers of culture. *People were dying and hearts were breaking.*

The news from Washington, D.C., and the Pentagon was nearly as grim. There, at least, the loss of life had been limited to the hundreds instead of the thousands, but this didn't ease the pain of those who would never see their loved ones again.

Then the gut-wrenching feelings that were by now all too

familiar were ratcheted even higher when news broke of a fourth plane that had crashed into a Pennsylvania field.

An emotional paralysis set in—the pain and shock were so great that we didn't dare yield to the feelings of loss, rage, and violation we knew were boiling within.

For many, a river of tears broke through at the first sight of brokenhearted firefighters and weeping police officers struggling to maintain their courage in the ashes of what once was. Others lost control when they glimpsed the gaunt faces of individual family members searching for any sign of their loved ones among the living.

PRAYING THE EMOTIONAL
DAM WOULD NEVER BURST

While rescue workers worked around the clock to sift through the ashes and rubble, agonizing hours stretched into days and the chances of survival grew less and less. Yet some family members still held on, hoping for the best and praying the emotional dam would never burst. They feared they couldn't survive its fury.

The truth is that tragedy seemingly visits every generation. The question is, How do we deal with it? Especially how, as Christians, do we deal with tragedy—not only tragedy in our lives, but also tragedy visited upon neighbors, whether near or far? Can we "mourn with those who mourn"? Is there purpose buried somewhere in the rubble?

The Christian response to tragedy of any proportion—whether it is the collapse of great towers or the collapse of a marriage—should be modeled after Jesus Christ's answers in a similar situation.

This was not the first time mighty towers in a leading metropolis have fallen and crushed the hopes of men and nations. Violent events and tragic deaths rocked another international city with a preeminent position on the world scene. Sometime after A.D. 32, a banner headline shocked Jerusalem citizens: "Tower Collapses, 18 Die!" Perhaps in the same year, another shocking headline had read, "Pilate Spills Blood of Worshippers in Temple Attack."[1]

WHAT DO YOU THINK ABOUT THIS, JESUS?

These first-century events seem especially relevant right now. Jesus was preaching to thousands of people about understanding right and wrong without hypocrisy when some people told Him about a tragedy that had just struck the city. They essentially said, *"What do You think about this, Jesus?"*

Now there were some present *at that time* who told Jesus about the Galileans whose blood Pilate had mixed with their sacrifices.

Jesus answered, "Do you think that these Galileans were worse sinners than all the other Galileans because they suffered this way? I tell you, no! But unless you repent, you too will all perish."[2]

These people weren't interested in the niceties and intricacy of theological meaning—they wanted to know how Jesus dealt with *current* events! They weren't posing some hypothetical problem in search of an equally hypothetical answer. They wanted to know then what millions of people want to know now: *How does God fit into all of this? Jesus, what do You think about it?*

TRAGEDY STRUCK ITS LARGEST AND MOST PROSPEROUS CITY

Jesus didn't dodge the question, but He did pull His answer from a previous day's headlines as well as from those that day. He said:

And what about the eighteen men who died when the Tower of Siloam fell on them? Were they the worst sinners in Jerusalem?[3]

Siloam was a well-known district or area in Israel's largest and most prosperous city, and it was a historic landmark called the "pool of Siloam." This pool was fed by an underground aqueduct dug centuries earlier during King Hezekiah's reign.

Evidently a tower of some kind collapsed and killed eighteen people in Siloam. It seems likely that the tower was part of the city's protective wall positioned close to the pool. Perhaps, as some speculate, Pilate's schemes were involved in the catastrophic failure of the wall that killed so many innocent victims.[4]

We don't know how many people lived in Jerusalem at that time, but even if only 100,000 people lived there, then the sudden and tragic deaths of 18 people would have the same comparative impact as the tragic loss of more than 5,000 people among New York City's 20 million inhabitants today.

Jesus was more interested in giving life and hope than the critics who wanted to point fingers of blame at innocent victims. He boldly pulled from the current events to establish the Kingdom of God in the midst of the collapsing kingdom of men.

There is no better time for Christian people to be like Jesus than when tragedy strikes their nation, their city, their neighborhood, or their own homes.

Many religious leaders seem to shrink back and disqualify themselves as voices of leadership and comfort in times of national tragedy. Still others blindly fall into the role of religious judges proclaiming to the hurting, "See, I *told* you so." Jesus didn't take advantage of tragedy to level blame; He drew from current events to bring direction, comfort, hope, and healing in times of need. We must do the same in spite of our personal pain.

CHAPTER 2

COMING HOME FROM A FUNERAL
(Opportunity Hides in Crises)

Tragedy and sorrow are painful, but they nearly always contain hidden opportunities for divine encounters that can transform the future. Isaiah the prophet described his personal encounter with the hidden opportunity of grief in his own words: *"In the year that King Uzziah died,* I saw the LORD sitting on a throne, high and lifted up, and the train of His robe filled the temple."[1]

Why is this so significant? What does it have to do with the pain we feel *today*? It may be the key you need to unlock your heart and find hope again. As I wrote in my book, *The God Catchers*:

How many times did this prophet walk into a temple before that unforgettable day when he "caught" God? . . .

. . . Isaiah's ministry spanned a period of forty years and the reign of as many as five different kings, but none of them equaled King Uzziah. It is no wonder Isaiah had an encounter with God in the temple—*he was just coming back from King Uzziah's funeral.*[2]

It seems that most Americans instinctively fall to their knees and take their pain to God when tragedy knocks. Nearly a half-century of "politically correct" foolishness and "separation of church and state" rhetoric fell into ruins just seconds after the first jet airliner crashed into the World Trade Center tower. Hardened network newscasters suddenly spoke of prayer and God in one breath while Congress convened a prayer meeting—unthinkable events just one tragedy earlier in America's history.

Some of us still remember the heartache that seized the nation on Sunday, December 7, 1941, after Pearl Harbor suffered an unexpected and unprovoked sneak attack by Japanese forces that killed 2,403 Americans, including 68 civilians, and wounded 1,178.[3] President Franklin D. Roosevelt said that day would "live in infamy," and he was right, but no one dared to believe a worse day or a more tragic loss of life would come our way.

Many more remember the shock they felt the day an assassin's bullets violently snuffed out the life of President John F.

Kennedy while he waved to American citizens lining the streets of Dallas, Texas, from an open convertible during a presidential motorcade on November 22, 1963.

I sense an urgent priority in the spirit realm—the Holy Spirit of God is speaking to you and to me. He is speaking volumes to a nation in pain. God is waiting to meet us on our way home from the funeral. The One who said, "Blessed are those who mourn, for they shall be comforted" fully intends to comfort us personally if we make the effort to detour from our road of grief to search for Him.[4]

Let me ask you a personal question: Did you come to God because things were going so well in your life that you just had to find someone to thank for it? Or did you come to Him in the middle of crisis? What was it that sparked your turn to God?

Opportunity hides in the middle of a crisis. I often conduct a "hand poll" in meetings attended by thousands of people with the same set of questions. The answer is invariably the same. The truth is that most if not all of us come to God in moments of crisis. Divine opportunity often hides in the middle of human crises.

I've noticed that whenever my kids get hurt, they insist that *Daddy* fix their "boo-boos." It isn't because my wife isn't a skilled healer or comforter, and it isn't because my children love me more than their mother. The reason is much more basic:

My children know that I will stretch out the treatment and make it last as long as possible. They think all of the parental fussing and the extravagant love and comfort is for them, but it's really for me. I milk the opportunity for loving parental intimacy with my children.

Our heavenly Father may not cause the "boo-boos" of life, but He will take every opportunity to spend precious moments in divine intimacy with us. Sometimes the only way He can gain access to our busy lives is to meet us "going home from a funeral."

We are never more tender than when going home from a funeral. Perhaps you have noticed that the hardest time doesn't come during the slow processional from the memorial service or mortuary to the cemetery. There is something oddly comforting about the line of cars traveling together in solemn procession with their lights on. At the very least, we feel "joined" in our grief as we huddle together at the burial site.

The hard times don't become apparent until after the memorial meal or "wake" is over and all of the people are gone. Once the mourners scatter and you begin the solitary drive home, silence blankets your heart and the reality of your loss sets in.

Most of us came to God after the death of something dear, or after we lost a loved one to death. For some it was the death of a dream; for others it was the death of a relationship or the sudden ending of a career. Perhaps it was the promise of a child's future being shattered by stark reality.

Nearly always, we began our search for Him after something awakened a crisis response in us. The journey to wholeness began when our brokenness made us realize that we have nowhere else to go. It was in the moment of crisis that we suddenly found God's address; in our pain His grace led our fingers to the long forgotten "business card" of Divine Love in our pockets.

Suddenly we said to ourselves, *This is where I can go. Now I remember; He said that whenever there was trouble, I could find Him.* It is in the very process of running to God in a crisis that we realize how often we run *from* brokenness when God runs *to* brokenness. Scripture says, "The LORD is near to those who have a broken heart."[5]

Why is it that we avoid the very intersection where God said He would always meet us? Whenever there is earthly brokenness there is always heavenly openness, but we don't like that address.[6] We avoid pain, brokenness, and personal failure at all costs. We don't want to go there because that is not a nice part of town. We would rather live on the proverbial "Easy Street."

The truth is you rarely find God on Easy Street because most of its residents believe they don't need Him. At the height of their human strength and personal achievements, they boldly thumb their noses at God and those who serve Him. The place most of us find God is on "Skid Row." It is the spiritual landing zone for people who have come face to face with their failures, weaknesses, frailty, and loneliness.

It is no accident that most of us found God when things were skidding out from under us. Most of us don't slow down enough to look up until our future looks bleak and the promise of tomorrow is being snatched from our "today." This is the moment of awakening, the point at which you see Him "high and lifted up." This is the moment of truth when suddenly you say, "I'm running to the Rock. The name of the Lord is a strong tower! I am running to the Tower that will never fall."[7]

This is the season of the towers, when men run from the crumbling towers of humanity and run to the High Tower for refuge and safety. Human crises birth divine opportunity, and God is patiently waiting to meet us on our way home from the funeral.

CHAPTER 3

WHAT IS IN YOUR POCKET?
(This Is No Time for Judgment)

In times of crisis, an army of armchair prophets and self-appointed religious regulators seem to have an especially fierce struggle with what I call the "Aha! spirit." Its most prominent symptom is the nearly uncontrollable urge to point a bony finger at people in distress and say, "See? I told you so!"

It reminds me of the would-be robber in comedy movies or in stories of a stickup gone awry. The thief pulls a finger from his pocket and jabs it in the back of his unsuspecting victim, hoping that the person will believe there is a real gun in his back. The mugging proceeds without a hitch as long as the farce goes smoothly, but once the truth is known, it is "open hunting season" for the weaponless mugger.

Jesus was dealing with a group of finger-pointing religious muggers when He was asked to comment on Pilate's murder of Galilean worshippers. It is clear from His reply that He knew they wanted Him to take a judgmental stand against the victims who died.

These men probably hoped this great teacher would make a public pronouncement about the obvious existence of some horrible sin in the victims' lives (and recognize the religious accusers' superior wisdom and righteous status in the process).

In their narrow view, sin and the harsh judgment it deserves were the only logical reason for the Galileans' tragic deaths, but Jesus quickly turned the tables on them. Why? He knew they didn't have any biblical or moral authority to make such claims. He said:

"Do you think those Galileans were worse sinners than other people from Galilee?" he asked. "Is that why they suffered? Not at all! And you will also perish unless you turn from your evil ways and turn to God. And what about the eighteen men who died when the Tower of Siloam fell on them? Were they the worst sinners in Jerusalem? No, and I tell you again that unless you repent, you will also perish."[1]

If God were to reward us solely on the basis of our "goodness" or "sinfulness," we literally wouldn't have a prayer. We should thank God that He doesn't. The only One who could declare that such victims were suffering purely because they were sinners and make it stick was God Himself. Yet Jesus would have none of it.

In fact, I read somewhere that ". . . God so loved the world that he gave his one and only Son, that whoever believes in him shall not perish but have eternal life. For God did not send his Son into the world to condemn the world, but to save the world through him."[2]

WILL YOU EXTEND A BONY
FINGER OR AN OPEN HAND OF LOVE?

What is in *your* pocket right now? Is your hand balled into a tight fist in fear or anger? Are you ready to extend that bony finger of accusation at the "guilty" or extend the open hand of unconditional love and compassion to the hurting and needy?

There is a time and season for everything,[3] and each person must make an eternal decision concerning the Lordship and divinity of Jesus Christ, the Son of God. We will all stand before the Righteous Judge someday, but too many of us act as if it is *our* job to judge others. The truth is that you will never meet a mere man or woman who qualifies for that role.

Have you noticed that Jesus delivered His strongest rebukes and judgments to religious people rather than sinners? The sinners knew they had sinned and didn't pretend otherwise. Religious people, however, sometimes feel they have earned a special place in God's realm even though God says everybody has sinned.

Jesus rarely if ever condemned sinners who wanted to be with Him. He didn't need to. His love and holiness did the work—they were drawn to Him so strongly that they were prepared to do whatever it took to remain with Him and please Him. They didn't desire to be good because they had to; they sought to be good because they wanted to.

THE BEST ANSWER TO CRISIS
SPRINGS FROM *OUR* REPENTANCE

When a crisis hits a life, a home, a city, or a nation, that is not the time for Christians to point their fingers and say, "You need to repent—we *told* you this would happen." The real truth is that the best response in a crisis isn't rooted in the world's repentance; it springs from *our* repentance. How can that be?

Listen to the words of God, who made this statement to King Solomon and the Israelites . . . and to all God Chasers who would hear the promise in the centuries that would follow:

> If My people who are called by My name will humble themselves, and pray and seek My face, and turn from their wicked

ways, then I will hear from heaven, and will forgive their sin and heal their land.[4]

As Christians, we must learn how to raise our voices with more than just accusation. If we read the Scripture passage correctly, God did not say He would forgive our sin and heal our land if the *world* repents. He specifically said, "If *My people* who are called by *My name* will humble themselves. . . ." In other words, God is saying we have something hidden in our pockets to offer to the world. What would that be?

Society at large does not have access to the key to revival. Rather, it is hidden within the pockets of the Christian family. Each of us is like a cosmic janitor who has so many keys that he has forgotten what some of them are for. We keep fumbling at the locks of spiritual and physical bondage and crushing grief that are imprisoning individuals and the nation.

While we fumble with the keys of life and point the finger of religious hypocrisy at others, God is waiting to see us accurately represent Him to the hurting people around us. He entrusted heaven's keys of freedom and wholeness to us, and He gave us the right words to bring healing as well as powerful declarations to set captives free.[5]

MAKE SURE YOU ASK THE RIGHT QUESTION

Since the keys to freedom, healing, and wholeness for the land are in our possession through Christ, the real question isn't, When will *God* do something about all of this? Right questions produce right answers. The right question is, When will *we* do something about it?

We may never have a more opportune time in this or any other century to present the reality of Jesus Christ and God's unconditional love to our hurting world. We have to find our voices and speak up.

America is coming home from a funeral, and hearts are tender like never before in this nation. There is no better time to talk to your neighbors and coworkers than right now.

SPEAK WITH THE RIGHT
VOICE AND PURE MOTIVES

You must find your voice and speak to the people you've been afraid to talk to all of these years. Just make sure you speak with the right voice and with pure motives, or you may cause your fellow Christians to be wrongly stereotyped and pigeon-holed as religious and hypocritical bigots. This is the exact place where Satan has always wanted us to stay.

My father, T. F. Tenney, sent me these words he had penned for those under his spiritual care shortly after the attack on the World Trade Center and the Pentagon:

It's time for the church to rise up and be counted. It's time for us to say to those whose grief has receded yet left them more aware than ever before of the aching void in their hearts and lives that we know the only One who is able to heal and fill them. As some will be left with a fearfulness about the future, we need to bring them to the One who holds tomorrow in His hand. To those who walk without hope, we need to find them and give them eternal hope and help.

Author Max Lucado, one of the best-known voices in the modern Christian world, offered an unforgettable prayer that was broadcast live on John Maxwell's Team Simulcast four days after the deadly attacks on the World Trade Center and the Pentagon. In the final moments of the prayer, Max prayed:

Most of all, do again what You did at Calvary. What we saw here last Tuesday [September 11, 2001], You saw there that Friday. Innocence slaughtered. Goodness murdered. Mothers weeping. Evil dancing. Just as the smoke eclipsed our morning, so the darkness fell on Your Son. Just as our towers were shattered, the very Tower of Eternity was pierced. And by dusk, heaven's sweetest song was silent, buried behind a rock. But You did not waver, O Lord. You did not waver. After three days in a dark hole, You rolled the rock and rumbled the earth and turned the darkest Friday into the brightest Sunday. Do it again, Lord. Grant us a September Easter.

Let Your mercy be upon our president, vice president, and their families. Grant to those who lead us wisdom beyond their years and experience. Have mercy upon the souls that departed and the wounded who remain. Give us grace that we might forgive and faith that we might believe. And look kindly upon Your church. For two thousand years You've used her to heal a hurting world.

Do it again, Lord. Do it again.

WHEN TOUGH MEN ARE MADE TENDER

On September 11, we found ourselves in a season when tough men were made tender, when it was common to see the most macho of men—firefighters and police officers—crying together in the ashes of yesterday's dreams. Presidents were praying and even Yankee Stadium was filled with the prayers of the bereaved instead of the cheers of exultant fans.

As I write these words, I am reminded of the statistical evaluation that there are only six degrees of separation from one human to any other human on earth. Some unknown villager in China may be only six relationships removed from you this very moment . . . but tragedy visits every home.

Sometimes the force of life's pain hits us all at once in one great collective blow. Our predecessors are familiar with the blows that struck our nation on December 7, on November 22, and most recently on September 11.

At other times tragedy visits us one soul at a time in the form of terminal cancer, a collision with a drunk driver, the news that a beloved parent has fallen to a massive heart attack, or the heartbreak of miscarriage and the new nursery doomed to remain empty.

WHAT DO YOU DO WHEN TRAGEDY STRIKES?

What does the Christian do when tragedy strikes his or her neighborhood? Worse than that, what do you do when disaster crashes into your own backyard? How do you recover from the tailspin of life when tragedy strikes your own home?

What do you do when the man next door or the daughter of the family across the street has died? What do you do when your neighbor's son is struck down in the bombing of the

Federal Building in Oklahoma City, or when your boss's daughter dies in the savage suicide attack on the World Trade Center towers?

There is a certain season when you plant—you can't sow seeds when the ground is hard; you sow when the ground is broken up. This is the season for Christians to sow seeds of compassion and love, not judgment. The hurting don't just live in New York; they also live next door. Every neighborhood is mourning. . . .

We need an army of "trained voices" in the land. God has one waiting in the wings if they will but answer His call. Isaiah described the "trained voice" of God's representative this way:

> The Sovereign LORD has given me his words of wisdom, so that
> *I know what to say to all these weary ones.* Morning by morn-
> ing he wakens me and opens my understanding to his will.[6]

We must understand that the One who sent us on this earthly mission of mercy is serious about the role we've taken upon ourselves in His name. Again, Jesus said, "God did not send his Son into the world to condemn the world, but to save the world through him."[7]

This is what you and I were born for. In the words of

Mordecai spoken to Queen Esther long ago, "Yet who knows whether you have come to the kingdom for such a time as this?"[8]

What is in your pocket? It is time for each of us to take off our judge's robe. We have no right to stand in judgment with clenched fists and pointed fingers hidden in our robes when we hold the keys of revival and restoration in our own pockets.

CHAPTER 4

WE DON'T KNOW
WHAT TO DO
(But Our Eyes Are upon You)

If you have ever witnessed a rescue operation at a car crash scene or watched news reports about emergency crews, then you know that ambulance personnel at an accident don't waste time trying to assign blame—they just want to bandage the wounds and preserve life. If life is preserved, the details can be sorted out later. We should remember that the emergency room is not a courtroom and the day of crisis is not necessarily the day of judgment.

We are heaven's emissaries of healing, Divinity's spiritual EMTs (Emergency Medical Technicians) sent to comfort the brokenhearted. The last time I heard, heaven's shelves still have plenty of medicine. God simply wants to know who is willing to apply the balm of Gilead, God's healing anointing to the world's wounds.

It seems to me that too many spiritual paramedics have dropped God's care package of love and grace and exchanged their uniforms of mercy for the robes of self-appointed judges—while trying to exonerate themselves from repentance and judgment in the process. Sorry, that job description isn't in God's Word.

If *our* repentance is the real key to revival and healing in our land, then I choose to posture myself, as a Christian, in the mode of repentance. This position of humility gives me the credibility to speak the words of healing to others. It gives me my "voice" in the world.

The problem is that when we speak with the wrong voice, we reinforce the unbiblical stereotype that Christians are accusers more than healers. In God's Book, only Satan and judgmental religious hypocrites are known as the accusers of the brethren. (Evidently God has reserved a special punishment for this destructive class of zealot.[1])

The biblical character Job demonstrated the ability to react with both the right attitude and the right voice when trusted with a tragedy. Even after losing his wealth, his children, and his health in just one day, the Bible says, "In all this Job did not sin with his lips."[2] He not only had a right attitude, he also spoke with a right voice. Job said, "Though *He* slay me, yet will I trust Him."[3] Job went to the worst possible scenario and settled the question. If you do this as well, nothing can shake your trust—not even tragedy.

HE REFUSED TO YIELD TO THE "AHA! SPIRIT"

Calamity fell on Job and his family for no apparent cause or reason, yet he refused to yield to the "Aha! spirit" and level blame at God or at the other people in his life. Jesus said:

> But I tell you: Love your enemies and pray for those who persecute you, that you may be sons of your Father in heaven. He causes his sun to rise on the evil and the good, and sends rain on the righteous and the unrighteous."[4]

It seems reasonable to me to assume that Job's response to tragedy in other people's lives was no different than his response to the tragedy in his own life. He blessed the Lord no matter what circumstance he faced in life.[5]

In the days following the tragic attacks on the World Trade Center and the Pentagon, Americans watched on national television as the members of Congress convened, not to legislate or debate over their differences, but to *deliberate and declare their dependency*. This wasn't a Congressional committee meeting; it was a congressional prayer meeting!

The scene reminded me of the scriptural passage where King Jehoshaphat of Judah found his nation surrounded by two armies that had been joined by forces from a third ally.

OUR EYES ARE ON YOU

This king's first act wasn't to convene a council of war or call a public debate on the matter. Instead, he called a national prayer meeting and asked the people to fast and pray to God for deliverance. This is what he prayed:

> O our God, will you not judge them? For we have no power to face this vast army that is attacking us. *We do not know what to do, but our eyes are upon you.*[6]

The truth is that when someone is born into this world, trouble comes with the territory. Even people who set their hearts to please God will face problems. I read that after Paul the apostle described how God had delivered him from every trap, ambush, and secret plot devised against him, he added with blunt honesty, "Everyone who wants to live a godly life in Christ Jesus will be persecuted."[7]

Trouble may come to a nation in the form of a collapsing banking industry, uncontrollable inflation, or a sudden rise in the national unemployment rate.

As individuals, we face trouble in countless forms, including shrinking financial resources, fractured marriage relationships, prodigal sons and daughters, and catastrophic diseases and accidents. How do you deal with trouble and crisis? Do you live in fear or in faith?

When secular strength dissipates, spiritual strength often grows stronger. If hope deferred makes the heart sick, then hope conferred makes the heart strong.[8]

A FUTILE HUNT FOR
HOPE IN THE SECULAR FOREST

When tragedy strikes you or those around you, the desperate hunt for hope in the secular forest is futile. The hunters invariably go home empty-handed and brokenhearted because humanity doesn't have the answers. Jesus gave us the answer in one of the most direct and unequivocal statements ever made: "I am the way, the truth, and the life. No one comes to the Father except through Me."[9]

The number of scriptural quotes that poured forth after crisis hit New York is simply incredible. I haven't ever heard an

American president quote so many Scriptures in my lifetime. God's Word has even found its way into national news broadcasts and onto the lips of normally aloof broadcasters.

Corporate prayer—the very action falsely portrayed as a dangerous affront to the Bill of Rights by the Supreme Court, federal court rulings, and various legislative motions—is now commonplace in the hallowed halls of Congress and the White House. How long has it been since Congress so corporately and with great conviction convened for a prayer meeting?

If you ever wonder what is going on, picture a nation in the painful process of going home from a funeral. So many pray in times of crisis.

In desperation we turned away from our false sources of strength because they failed us in the hour of crisis. A few determined madmen armed with simple box cutters did what the combined military might of multiple nations failed to do in World Wars I and II. In less than seventy minutes, they effectively overwhelmed America's advanced technology and military might, dealing a tragic blow to our economic clout and fierce marketing and financial expertise.

Our traditional sources of strength and security seemingly collapsed upon themselves with the fall of the World Trade Center towers, leaving us with only the bitter smell of ash and the smoldering remains of our dreams and labor. A tragedy of these proportions often leaves people wandering aimlessly, looking for direction on where to go and what to do.

Where do people go when they have nowhere else to go? To whom do you run in times of crisis? Crisis is turning our nation back to the Answer of the ages—God.

SOMEONE MUST GIVE AN ANSWER

Although we don't want to seem opportunistic, we do want to share what God has given to us when the opportunity presents itself. When brokenness and hunger for hope are evident in a neighbor, a family member, or a nation, someone must give them the answer. If you and I do not give hurting people an answer when they wallow in the pain of their brokenness and mourning, then they will awake to a cold dawn of hopelessness. About the only thing worse than brokenness is hopelessness.

In times of tragedy someone must step to the front and give a voice of hope. When you are going home from a funeral, you clutch at any words that offer hope to your heart's unanswered questions.

There is nothing more frustrating than dealing with someone in grief and not knowing what to say.

I was glued to the television for two weeks after the jetliners plunged into the World Trade Center towers, the Pentagon, and the soil of Pennsylvania. Like so many other American citizens, I hung on every word just listening for hope and looking for an answer.

THEY WERE JUST POSTURING . . .

It didn't take long to realize that no matter who was doing the talking, no one in the long line of experts and credentialed officials parading across America's television screens really knew what to say. Most were sincere and deeply troubled by the events of September 11, but when it came to issues of hope and healing, they were just posturing.

No matter how often I switched from channel to channel and network to network, all I found was more hand wringing and finger-pointing. No one had any answers for America's broken heart.

Now is the time for Christians to stand up in the vacuum of postulating voices. We need to stand up in Christ, find our voices, and say what needs to be said. God is out to commission you or send you on a mission as an agent of Divinity.[10]

There has never been a better time for you to talk to people about God. People who would normally refuse to talk with you about God will seek you out in the months and years ahead. Even those people who wouldn't give you the time of day before tragedy struck will find themselves drawn to you when you open your Bible. Miraculously, they will sit down and open their hearts when you say, "Have you ever read this? What do you think of that?"

The unprecedented crisis that gripped America and the world in September of 2001 also created a season of unprecedented openness in the hearts of people. This is no time for us to go back to "church as usual." We cannot afford to become like secular society and wring our hands in despair while abandoning our voices in a vacuum of unbelief and fear.

Yes, we are still real people who feel all of the emotions others feel in times of tragedy, death, pain, and loss. Yet we serve a mighty God who is real and well able to lead us through any valley of death or discouragement.

COMING HOME FROM THE FUNERAL
OF THEIR INNOCENCE AND DREAMS

You and I must understand that what the world needs after a crisis is a friend. Our neighbors, our government officials and business leaders, our associates and fellow plant workers have been to a funeral. They are coming home from the funeral of their innocence and dreams; they've just buried their hopes for safety and self-sufficiency.

These people need someone to go home with them who has the right words to say at the right time. Now more than ever, they need a caring friend to gently guide them to the Rock who is higher than their pain and sorrow. They need a loving voice rooted in the Rock of Ages to tell them the story of Jesus, who said:

Come to me, all you who are weary and burdened, and I will give you rest. Take my yoke upon you and learn from me, for I am gentle and humble in heart, and you will find rest for your souls.[11]

We talked about *credibility* and linked it to *repentance* in this chapter, but do you understand the connection? If we as Christians repent before God, He can change our hearts and give us true compassion for hurting people. That compassion for others then gives us true credibility with the outside world.

GOD AND MAN ARE SEARCHING FOR "A VERY UNUSUAL ENVIRONMENT"

Jesus appeared to be as comfortable with sinners as He was with saints. I think it was because He genuinely loved them all. In the book, *Chasing God, Serving Man*, I described the unique relationship of credibility in the world with our relationship with God:

. . . real revival is when both God and man show up at the same time and the same place. That can happen only when you have *credibility in both realms.* You must have enough credibility in the human realm to make man feel comfortable, and you must have credibility in the divine realm to make God feel comfortable.

. . . The Church is usually a little unbalanced because it is constantly torn between the practical and the spiritual. Most churches tend to lean toward one side or the other; they are either *socially active* or *spiritually passionate.* Very seldom do you find a church that manages to be *both,* and when you do, you have found a very unusual environment.[12]

Nations and individuals in crisis need anointed bridge builders who know how to lead entire funeral processions across the river of despair and into God's loving care. Hurting and wounded people are desperate for answers to their paralyzing pain and dulling despair.

God has given us more than a theoretical solution or an intellectual thought process. We can offer more than a therapy program or some experimental painkiller for the soul—we are authorized to offer them healing and hope through the Way, the Truth, and the Life.[13]

CHAPTER 5

WHY DO I FEEL SO WEAK?
*(Discerning he Difference Between
a Resource and the Source)*

How often have you heard people caught in the maelstrom of a crisis say, "All of a sudden I feel weak in the knees"? It's not uncommon for people in these situations to actually faint.

I remember experiencing that same feeling while watching news reports of the tragic events unfolding at the World Trade Center and the Pentagon. After several days of nonstop tension and consecutive trips on the heartrending emotional roller coaster of the tragedy, I finally turned away from my television and asked myself the question, Why do I feel so weak? The rhetorical answer came quickly from deep within my being: *I feel as if I just came home from a funeral.*

The passage from Isaiah 6:1 immediately came to mind: "In

the year that King Uzziah died. . . ." Yet, this time I could almost *feel* the pain the prophet must have felt the day he wandered into the temple on his way home from a funeral. I felt the same way.

Most of us rush past the simple statement Isaiah penned about that day so we can move ahead to the "good part" about the mighty seraphim, the shaking of the temple foundations, and the smoke that filled that place of worship.

Somehow we associate this overlooked Scripture passage with the historical "begats" or the detail-laden Levitical laws and regulations found elsewhere in the Bible. For the most part, we assume this great prophet somehow remained unmoved and untouched by the death of his cousin-king, Uzziah. In our minds, the first sentence in the chapter has somehow become an unread and essentially invisible foreword that exists solely to lead us to the really exciting material.

HIS WORDS CARRIED EMOTIONAL
WEIGHT AND PERSONAL SORROW

I'm convinced Isaiah was in the depths of the weak-kneed, bro-kenhearted mourning process the day he wandered into that temple and had a divine encounter with the God of eternity. I suspect Isaiah's introductory words, "In the year that King Uzziah died, I saw the Lord . . ." carry far more emotional weight and personal sorrow than most of us can imagine.

Think of the times a friend or relative has said to you, "It has been two years since my husband died . . ." or "Do you remember when you took this picture of us together? . . . It's hard to believe she has been gone for six years."

How can any of us really understand and comprehend the personal pain encapsulated in brief statements like these unless we have experienced something similar in our own lives?

This was a season of mourning for Isaiah, and the saga of his pain had two roots: the loss of King Uzziah in death and Isaiah's own loss of hope, personal security, and close companionship.

Isaiah was actually King Uzziah's cousin, and it may be assumed he was the official court preacher of the kingdom. Perhaps for years Isaiah had been the prophet of choice, the preacher of prestige, and the man of the moment. He was the king's highly favored designated hitter, the holy man who always prayed at the inaugurations and official state functions.

As a presumed family member of royal blood, Isaiah was the preeminent spiritual leader whom King Uzziah consistently chose above all other candidates to preside over the spiritual emphasis at every royal event and national celebration. As long as Cousin Uzziah ran things, Isaiah knew he would hold first place as the favored preacher of that family lineage.

DISCONNECTED FROM THE SOURCE

There seems to be a clear distinction between the prophetic ministry of Isaiah *before* Uzziah's death and his writings *after* his cousin had died and the prophet saw the glory of the Lord. Why is that? Because sometimes we disconnect our prosperity from its true source.

At times we become disconnected by thinking our prosperity occurred because of our own ingenuity. We also may fall into the delusion that we earned our prosperity through our own strength and abilities, forgetting in a flash of dangerous amnesia that every breath and every minute we enjoy apart from pain and sickness is a precious gift from the God of life.

Even Isaiah the prophet was just a man. He entered the world through a womb like any other human being. He had to eat food and drink fluids regularly or he would die. He knew the full gamut of human emotions and experiences, including happiness, sadness, fear, anticipation, disappointment, and the heartbreak of sorrow.

Is it possible that the Isaiah who ministered in the king's court before Uzziah's death was leaning—just a little, at least—on the arm of his royal cousin as well as on the provision and presence of God?

We need to understand that prosperity ultimately comes

from God. Even the most sincere God Chasers may mistakenly lean on the false arm of human strength if they fail to understand the difference between their *resources* and their *Source*.

Our ministry has grown quite rapidly over the past few years. We mushroomed from a modest five-person office into an international ministry with forty full-time employees and a growing number of interns working at high speed to keep up with the needs pouring in. Sometimes we go through seasons when we need more income just to cover our outgo for special ministry outreach projects.

NEVER MISTAKE MERE OUTLETS
FOR THE TRUE SOURCE OF POWER

I have to remind the staff and our ministry partners that we must depend on God as our Source rather than the people whom He sends us as His resources of prayer support and financial supply. When things get tight, we don't need to collect bigger offerings or make better "offers" for those who financially support the ministry. Although people may be our resource, they are not our Source. God alone is our unfailing Source.

What is the difference between a resource and a source? One of the best illustrations may be as close to you as the nearest electrical appliance. Hundreds of times a week, people plug in to electrical outlets to operate their kitchen appliances, television sets, radios, hair dryers, and countless other electrical devices. We don't think much about it, but when asked, many people would point at those electrical outlets and say, "There is the source of power."

In reality, if you want to find the true source of that power, you will have to trace the electrical wires through conduits and power boxes until you find the main circuit breaker and electrical box elsewhere in the building.

If you keep tracing the flow of power, the trail will ultimately lead you to a central power grid and take you all the way back to a hydroelectric dam, a coal-fired or petroleum-fueled electrical generator plant, or a nuclear power facility—the generating *source* of the electricity.

JUST TRACE THE POWER ALL
THE WAY BACK TO CALVARY'S STREAM

The same kind of confusion takes place in churches and Christian meetings every day. Sometimes people look at a gifted preacher behind a pulpit and say, "I want to connect to *that* source of power." No, they don't understand what they're saying. That preacher may be an outlet or resource for divine power, but if you really want to connect to the *Source* of that power, you must trace the red blood that flows all the way back to Calvary's stream. (Even the apostle Paul had to deal with the misplaced worship of people in Lystra who thought he was the Greek god Hermes.[1])

Isaiah was disconnected from his earthly resource and forced to search for the true Source of life. Just because the brook dried up doesn't mean the river has run dry, but it probably feels that way. How do you recover from such a devastating blow? How do you pray when you have no tears left to shed and your strength is nearly gone? Perhaps that is the time to pull out the "ABC Prayer."

HE CAN PUT THE WORDS TOGETHER

A friend told me a story he has used for years to illustrate the way God helps us pray when our "pray-er" is just worn out:

> There was a little girl who was staying with her grandparents. When it was time for her to go to bed her grandfather told her that he would come to her room in a moment to say her prayers with her.
>
> As he came to the doorway he realized she had already started praying, but he was a bit puzzled. He overheard her saying her ABC's. As she went through the alphabet, she was

saying each letter with great emphasis. Finally, she concluded with some thank-yous and her amen, and proceeded to get into bed.

When her grandfather came to tuck her in, he said, "Darling, I listened to your prayers. It sounded like you were praying your ABC's." She responded with this explanation: "Yes, Grandpa, I just had so much to pray about, and I am such a little girl that I don't know all the words. But I knew that if I gave Him the whole alphabet, He could put the words together."

This little girl was closer to the truth than she knew. I read somewhere that ". . . the Spirit helps us in our weakness. We do not know what we ought to pray for, but the Spirit himself intercedes for us with groans that words cannot express."[2]

The man called Paul who rose from the dust of the Damascus road after being blinded by Divine Light was a different man than the one who stormed out of Jerusalem on a man-authorized mission to persecute Christians in Syria's largest city.[3] As I wrote about Paul's transformation in *The God Catchers*: "Never underestimate the power of one moment in His presence. Thirty seconds in the manifest presence of God turned a murderer named Saul into a martyr named Paul."[4]

HE SAW THE LORD AND WAS CHANGED

What happened to Isaiah the brokenhearted prophet, the mourning family member who staggered into the temple bearing all the burdens of tragic loss and an uncertain future? He saw the Lord. It is safe to say that the man who left the temple wasn't the same man who entered it earlier:

Read the first five chapters of the book of Isaiah, and notice their context and content. They say, "Woe is me . . . woe is you . . . and woe is everybody."

Then he had the God encounter noted in Isaiah 6.

After that, there are sixty more chapters of incredible prophetic declarations. Not "woe is me and woe is you," but He was "high and lifted up" and "unto us a Son is given" and "the government will be upon His shoulder" and "Wonderful, Counselor, Mighty God, Everlasting Father."

What's the difference? *If you ever see Him, it changes everything.*[5]

The weight of sorrow, the shock of a tragedy, and even the terror of imminent death can rob our bodies and minds of their wills to move, act, or pray. The best thing you can do in moments of such paralyzing weakness is pray and cry out to

Him in *any way you can*. Frankly, it doesn't take much to capture the attention of God.

Ask Stanley Praimnath, a church deacon and Sunday school superintendent from Elmont, Long Island, whose story is one of the many amazing testimonies emerging from the ashes of the twin World Trade Center towers.

AN UNUSUAL URGENCY INVADED HIS PRAYERS

All morning on Tuesday, September 11, Stanley had sensed an unusual urgency invade his normal prayer time. He prayed, "Lord, cover me and all my loved ones under Your precious blood." He said later, "Even though I said that and believed it, I said it over and over and over."

He was at his desk on the eighty-first floor of World Trade Center Two retrieving phone messages when he saw "fireballs" falling from World Trade Center One visible through his office window. When his call to the other building wouldn't go through, Stanley and another worker headed for the elevator.

They were joined by his company's president and CEO and they made it all the way down to the concourse level of the tower when a security guard told them, "Two World Trade is secure. Go back to your office."

Stanley went back to the eighty-first floor and heard his phone ringing as soon as he reached his office. It was someone from Chicago who asked if Stanley "was watching the news." Praimnath assured the caller everything was fine and looked up to see United Air Lines Flight 175 heading straight for his building.

"All I can see is this big gray plane, with red letters on the wing and on the tail, bearing down on me," Stanley said. "But this thing is happening in slow motion. The plane appeared to be like one hundred yards away. I said, 'Lord, You take control; I can't help myself here.'"

Stanley's New Testament was on top of his desk, and somehow he knew the Lord would take care of him once he took shelter there. He curled into a fetal position under the desk just before Flight 175 pierced the side of World Trade Center Two and exploded.

It was a miracle that Stanley was unhurt because the jetliner had crashed into the tower just twenty feet away from his position. Yet, he knew he was still in serious trouble. He could see a wing from the jetliner engulfed in flames in his department's doorway, and he was still trapped under debris piled up to his shoulders.

LORD, YOU TAKE CONTROL

Instinctively, he prayed, "Lord, You take control, this is Your problem now," and an incredible strength flooded through his body.

The office was plunged in darkness due to the smoke and total loss of power as he continued to cry out and pray, "Lord, I have things to do. I want to see my family, Lord; help me through."

He suddenly saw the beam of a flashlight and clawed his way through debris to reach his "guardian angel," but every exit was blocked and a wall divided them. To make matters worse, Stanley couldn't breathe because of the fumes from the jet fuel and raging fire. Finally he dropped to his knees and prayed, "Lord, You've got to help me. You've brought me this far; help me to get to the staircase."

Then he called out to the man behind the wall, "There's one thing I've got to know—do you know Jesus?" When he learned the man went to church every Sunday, the two men prayed for the strength to break through the wall. Then they stood up and literally punched a hole in the wall that was large enough for Stanley to squeeze through.

Stanley and his "angel," an older man named Brian, began the long descent from the eighty-first floor. They went a floor at a time, checking each one to see if anyone was still there. They found an injured man on one floor and Stanley offered to carry him out, but a security guard advised them to send some-one up instead.

When they finally made it down to the concourse, the only

people they saw were firefighters who shouted to them, "Run, run, run!" Stanley said, "They were telling us to run out, but they were not concerned about themselves." Unfortunately, the concourse was already surrounded by fire by that time. They soaked their clothing with water from the building's sprinkler system, held hands, and ran through the flames toward the old Trinity Church building about two blocks away. "As soon as I held onto the gate of that church, the building [World Trade Center Tower Two] collapsed."[6]

Are you in a crisis and feeling your knees beginning to buckle? There is no better time to cry out to God than on your way home from a funeral. Although He would never bring evil upon you, "God will take advantage of your desperate feelings to create a dependence on Him."[7] In the aftermath of a tragedy, learn to trust.

CHAPTER 6

THE DEMISE OF A KING
(The Eulogy of Self-Dependence)

If Isaiah was feeling weak and vulnerable after facing tragedy, why do we think it so strange when we feel weak and vulnerable in the face of our own tragedies? You may not be mourning the loss of your king or president—it may be that your child was arrested, your job was eliminated due to downsizing, or your spouse decided the grass was greener on the other side of matrimony. A loved one may have perished during the unwelcome events of catastrophe, or perhaps an unfavorable medical report dashed your hopes for sharing another Christmas morning with your family.

The litany of personal tragedy is endless, and its pain is virtually universal. In spite of the apparent "what-goes-around-comes-around" nature of suffering, we still pretend it will never come our way while daily passing unspoken judgments on the vulnerabilities of other people—whether they wrestle with physical weakness, character flaws, or mental or physical impairment.

Why is it sometimes easier to make room in parking lots for physically impaired people than to make positive allowances in our own opinions for mentally impaired or socially dysfunctional people? Is one type of impairment somehow more politically correct than another? The truth is that despite our desperate efforts to dismiss the possibility, you and I are only one heartbeat or one birth from just such a crisis.

Where do you turn when you suddenly feel weak of heart and unsteady on your feet? What do you say to a friend whose knees appear to be buckling under the heavy strain of crisis? You will never know what to say if you don't know *who* or even *what* died.

Whose funeral was it? For Isaiah, it was King Uzziah. For Job, it was his wealth, then his children, and finally his health. (The adversary tried desperately to steal Job's faith as well, but failed.)

Sometimes we grieve over the demise of something other than a person. You may be mourning the death of a relationship, the termination of a job, the demise of a dream, or even the destruction of hope itself, but in each case, it is essential to know whose funeral it is, whose death is being mourned. We'll talk about that more in a moment.

ENSNARED BY FALSE ALLEGIANCES AND MISPLACED DEVOTION

We often create new problems or make existing problems worse through false allegiances and misplaced devotion. If you swear allegiance to the king of wealth, who becomes king when the economy collapses? If you swear allegiance to the king of health, who becomes king when health is deposed? If you swear sole allegiance to the fraternity of your family, what happens when time, differences, and disease take their tolls on your earthly idol?

Obviously, it isn't wrong to desire financial prosperity, good health, or healthy and loving family relationships. The problems come when we enthrone them in the temple of the heart and displace the true King of hearts in the process.

Job's wealth failed, his health was suddenly taken from him, and even his children were taken in death through sudden violence at the instigation of the ultimate terrorist. Yet, in spite of the unrelenting pain and loss, Job still said to himself and to his negative and judgmental friends: "'Naked I came from my mother's womb, and naked I will depart. The LORD gave and the LORD has taken away; may the name of the LORD be praised.' In all this, Job did not sin by charging God with wrongdoing."[1]

Even in the midst of his pain, Job boldly acknowledged that the lordship in his life was not of this world. His undying allegiance to God made that part of his being forever untouchable and impervious to the sorrows and tragedies of earth.

Sometimes, the heavenly King can be revealed only when earthly kings die. It is apparent that Isaiah loved and honored God, but his life and ministry took a dramatic turn after the death of King Uzziah. It was only after the prophet's earthly king died that he saw the heavenly King "sitting on a throne, high and lifted up."[2]

WE NEED TO UNDERSTAND
WHOSE FUNERAL IT IS

As I stated previously, we need to understand whose funeral it is, who or what has died, before we can understand our feelings in the midst of crisis. Only then can we answer the difficult questions that arise when we feel burdened beneath the pressure that a crisis can bring.

Who died in Isaiah's life? King Uzziah. So what do we know about this king who seemed so influential in the prophet's life? It seems he was an earthly king with tremendous accomplishments. The Bible contains a detailed eulogy and litany of King Uzziah's life accomplishments.[3]

- He assumed the throne of Judah at the *age of sixteen* and ruled for *fifty-two years*.

- Uzziah "warred against the Philistines." In other words, he boldly and aggressively confronted the perennial enemies to his nation and the safety of his people. He wasn't content to take a purely defensive posture when enemies endangered the safety of his people. He correctly identified the source of danger and then boldly took the battle to his enemy's front door.

- This king *"broke down the wall of Gath."* Perhaps the name *Gath* will mean more if we connect it to another, more famous name—Goliath. Goliath was a giant from Gath, a city known and feared as the hometown of giants. Uzziah clearly possessed such warlike abilities that he was strong enough to break down the wall of the "city of the giants." That means he not only pursued his enemies, but he also *made progress and defeated his enemies.* What an incredible accomplishment! If you were to introduce King Uzziah to an audience before he delivered a speech, you would have to say, "This is the man who broke down the wall of Goliath's hometown, the city of giants."

- This king didn't stop there. He even *built cities among his enemies!* It takes a secure man to build a city, but this man dared to build multiple cities. In fact, he was so unworried by his enemies that he dared to build those cities right in the middle of them! This leader won *territorial victories* over his enemies. He wasn't content to drive them out; he crossed their boundaries, seized their possessions, and built outpost cities right in front of their houses.

- The Bible says Uzziah was an *exceedingly strong king.* Even his enemies paid tribute and tax to him.

- King Uzziah was considered to be one of the *good kings* in the long list of rulers over Judah and Israel.

- He *strengthened Jerusalem.* That meant a great deal to God. The Bible still exhorts us to "pray for the peace of Jerusalem."[4] Thank God for kings and leaders who also strengthen the spiritual Jerusalem, the Church.

- Uzziah was also a wise manager and businessman. He *dug wells* and "*had much cattle.*" This is a picture of spiritual and natural provision. It also means this king loved husbandry and appreciated *the shepherding factor*. (We still need leaders who love and appreciate the shepherding factor.)

- This king had *many cunning warriors*. If a king wants to dare to break down the walls of the city of giants, then he had better surround himself with "cunning warriors," or strong and wise men of war.

- The Bible also says something really peculiar about this king. (It is the only time we see this statement in the Scriptures.) It says he *invented cunning engines of defense.* This leader carefully searched for better ways to protect what God had given his nation. We don't know that Uzziah was the first to do it, but one could speculate that he invented advanced catapult engines designed to shoot arrows and stones from towers and corner locations. We also may speculate that they were complicated and evidently effective enough to create envy among his enemies and warrant special mention in the Scriptures.

Then we come upon a Bible passage that gives us the home address of the beginning of King Uzziah's end. The eulogy abruptly ends with this simple statement: "He was marvelously helped till he became strong."[5]

As human beings, we run into serious problems every time we mistake our resources for our Source. I'm convinced this principle applies to nations, churches, and families as much as it does to individuals. The Bible says something about King Uzziah that has eternal importance: ". . . *as long as he sought the LORD*, God made him prosper."[6]

BEWARE PROSPERITY
DISCONNECTED FROM ITS SOURCE

For years I've sensed a growing concern for this nation every time I pull out a coin. We know that as long as King Uzziah sought the Lord, God made him prosper. Our nation's coins bear the inscription, "In God We Trust." Yet it seems that more and more of us have really come to believe our prosperity is something *we* created. In essence, our nation's prosperity is rapidly becoming disconnected from its true Source.

In my heart, it feels as though we have taken a big eraser and are rubbing away the inscription to replace it with a more truthful but very dangerous statement: "In Money We Trust." I'm convinced I'm not alone. More and more Christians seem to be worried that America has begun to mistake her resources for *the*

Source. I just can't shake the reverberating truth in the words, "As long as he sought the LORD, God made him prosper."

Something happened to King Uzziah when he began to lean on his own strength, and none of us are immune from his disease of self-reliance. I understand the value of positive self-esteem and self-love. Even Jesus said we must love our brothers as we love ourselves; however, He never intended for us to shove aside God's throne to make room for our own throne in honor of King "ME."

CRISIS MAY COME SOONER TO THOSE
ASLEEP IN THE DOORWAY OF COMPLACENCY

I have found out that when I become foolish enough to think I am strong apart from God's grace and help, then that is when I am at my weakest and most vulnerable point. Each time prior to December 7, November 22, and September 11, our nation has been strong and in control in its own eyes. Does this mean America brought these three tragedies upon herself? No. Determined and terribly misled men fueled by blind hatred and demonic motivation brought tragedy to our homes in each case. Yet America clearly lay asleep in the doorway of complacency when each of these tragedies struck. As a nation, we were leaning heavily upon our own strength, and I'm sure that didn't help our situation.

It pays to continually remember and honor the truth we stamp on the coin of the realm: *In God We Trust*. According to the spiritual principle we see in King Uzziah's life, we will be marvelously helped by God *until* we think we are strong apart from Him.

Part of the problem may be that our society is teaching some half-truths as whole truths. It is true that God wants us to love ourselves, but most secular sources carefully avoid the greater requirement that precedes it. This is the *whole* truth:

> "Love *the Lord your God* with all your heart and with all your soul and with all your mind and with all your strength." The second is this: "Love your neighbor *as yourself.*" There is no commandment greater than these.[7]

Our society proclaims one truth above all others: "Follow your heart." We see it splashed on billboards, portrayed on movie screens and in TV dramas, projected in colorful posters and T-shirts, and expounded in countless self-help books, talk shows, and counseling manuals.

My advice is that you *don't* follow your heart. Contrary to popular theology, philosophy, and psychology, man is not "born innately good." My Bible says, "The heart is deceitful above all things and beyond cure. Who can understand it? I the LORD search the heart and examine the mind, to reward a man according to his conduct, according to what his deeds deserve."[8]

DON'T FOLLOW YOUR
HEART—FOLLOW *HIS* HEART

There is a cure for what ails us, however. The road map of the unredeemed human heart will only lead us down the blind alley of hopelessness. If we are going to follow something, we should follow *God's* heart revealed in the unwavering road map of His Word. The human heart—especially a heart in crisis—doesn't always know where it is going. I've learned through experience that God's Word ". . . is a lamp to my feet and a light for my path."[9]

- What has died in your life? What has died in the life of the nation?

- Was it our false sense of omnipotence?

- Was it an unconscious or conscious air of superiority?

- Was it our sense of invincibility gained over years of relative peace and safety without our national boundaries?

The truth is that we are flesh in a season of insecurity. We must do whatever it takes to return to a safe house, a safe place for our souls and our families. There is only one Strong Tower that will never fall or fail us. It's time to call on the name of the Lord, for "the name of the LORD is a strong tower; the righteous run to it and are safe."[10]

CHAPTER 7

PRESUMPTION IS A DEAD-END STREET
(Spiritual Arrogance Will Divert Your Divine Destiny)

Crisis has an amazing effect on the clarity of human discernment. If nothing else, a crisis reminds us that no matter who we are or what we have accomplished in life, each of us is only one catastrophe away from paralyzing weakness. If weakness and brokenness have the ability to lead us to God, then we should be warned that strength and arrogance may well lead us away from Him.

It is during our unwilling journey along the path of tragedy that most of realize how often we have walked into areas of life where God has placed warning signs that say "Keep Off the Grass" and "Don't Eat This Fruit."

This reminds me of an unforgettable "home video" clip I

saw aired on a national TV program showing the near-death experience of a young boy who leaned past the warning signs in a zoo. He accidentally fell into the gorilla enclosure and was in danger of being killed by gorillas in the area. Evidently they viewed the boy as a dangerous interloper because they repeatedly threatened to attack him.

Obviously a young boy, especially a child who has been injured in a fall, is no match for angry male gorillas. He most likely would have been killed very quickly except for one miraculous intervention.

For reasons known only to God, some primitive mothering instinct rose up in a female gorilla that was in the area, and she rushed over to the hurting young boy and sheltered him with her muscular arms. Each time the agitated male gorillas got too close, she waved them off with angry gestures and a no-nonsense appearance. Fortunately, zoo workers and volunteers were able to rescue the boy after a few minutes, but his real rescuer that day wasn't wearing a uniform.

As the scenes of that tense drama flashed across the nation's television sets, I wondered how many parents, zoo administrators, law enforcement officers, emergency rescue personnel, and liability insurance underwriters asked themselves: *How could this have been prevented? How many warning signs, bar-*

riers, fences, safety systems, and human guards did this child have to ignore to land among those gorillas?

Sometimes tragedy forces us to notice how many warning signs we have chosen to ignore. Anyone who has survived a hit-and-run accident after an unknown driver ran a stop sign will never again drive through an intersection without feeling a sense of dread. Most likely, he or she will never again be guilty of casually cruising through a stop sign, either. A crisis forever heightened that person's awareness of traffic warning signs.

THE KING RAN A STOP SIGN AND COLLIDED WITH DIVINITY'S THRONE

King Uzziah did fine until he ran a stop sign and collided with a throne higher than his own:

> So his fame spread far and wide, for he was marvelously helped till he became strong. But when he was strong *his heart was lifted up, to his destruction, for he transgressed against the LORD his God* by entering the temple of the LORD to burn incense on the altar of incense.[1]

The mighty king of Judah said to himself, "What is all of this spiritual protocol to me? These warning signs and consequences do not apply to me." Sometimes even spiritual people lose their way and begin to assume—or presume—that *earthly strength* is equivalent to *heavenly strength*. It is not.

Where did King Uzziah's heart lead him? It led him to destruction. Are you wondering why we are talking about his funeral when we just reviewed all of this great king's strengths?

THERE IS A DEADLY DIFFERENCE
BETWEEN IGNORANCE AND ARROGANCE

The answer is simple and painful: King Uzziah's strengths led him to arrogance, and his arrogance led him into spiritual trespassing. The definition of spiritual trespassing is not *"ignorance about boundary lines"* but *"arrogance about boundary lines."*

King Uzziah had been top dog in Judah for about half a century at that point. He was so strong, so feared by his enemies, and so beloved in the eyes of his subjects that he assumed he could walk anywhere he chose to walk. He didn't have to wait for anyone. This earthly king had authority to go anywhere and do anything—or so he thought.

One day he decided that he was tired of just going to worship services. He decided that he wanted to offer sacrifices to God and walk behind the veil in the temple as the high priest did once a year.

"I want to do what those priests up there are doing. I want to offer God the sweet incense, too. I am growing impatient with the pace of these priests. I think I will burn the incense myself."

King Uzziah had already enjoyed every other honor his nation had to offer; now he assumed he could take what no earthly nation had the authority to offer him.

"I am the king, after all. I can say anything and do anything I want. Remember, I have broken down the walls of the giants and built mighty cities right under the noses of my enemies. What is the barrier of this spiritual protocol to me? I don't have to pay any attention to these warnings—I am the anointed king over Judah."

DESTINY DECIDED IN
A MOMENT OF ARROGANCE

Unfortunately for King Uzziah, his destiny was decided in a moment of arrogance. Although the king could legally enter the temple of God, he entered the temple with arrogance in his heart. He acted in presumption on the basis of false strength that was totally disconnected from his true Source.

This wasn't the first time he had been in the temple or encountered the proper protocol of Old Testament Jewish worship there. He knew certain things were forbidden, but the Bible says he "transgressed against the LORD his God *by entering the temple of the LORD to burn incense* on the altar of incense."[2]

Let me jar your thinking just enough to push this picture in the here and now of life in the twenty-first century: This was a "saved" king. Uzziah was a good king; he wasn't an idol worshiper who rebelled against the plan of God all of his life. Yet, even "saved" kings can be strangers to behind-the-veil worship in the holy presence of God.

The real problem was that Uzziah had not been anointed for service in that realm. He had not submitted himself to the bloody process of covering the sins of the guilty with the blood of the innocent. To be authorized for burning incense, he would need to exchange his royal robes for priestly ephods—he would have to resign from being a king and become a priest!

Not just anybody could pass beyond the veil of separation and enter the Holy of Holies to burn incense before the Lord. It was a service that God Himself reserved for dedicated priests who had been surrounded by the blood of an innocent victim.

Before any descendent of Aaron ever dared to enter the Holy of Holies to minister in the holy presence of God, he made plenty sure there was innocent blood on his earlobes, on his thumbs, and on his toes. There was a priestly ephod on his breast and signs of a thorough preparation process in his heart.

DON'T FORGET THE ROPE—JUST IN CASE

The danger of carrying uncovered sin into the presence of God's absolute holiness was so serious that the other priests would tie a rope to the ankle of the priest chosen to enter the Holy of Holies each year—just in case something went wrong and he died on the spot. (The only way to safely remove the body from the Most Holy Place was to drag it out under the veil using the rope.)

It is as if this earthly king thought that his personal strength was omnipotent. It *still* takes the blood of the Lamb and a priestly bloodline to venture beyond the veil and into the presence of God. The only way to acquire these credentials is to be washed in the blood of the innocent Lamb of God and to receive a new family name and a priestly bloodline through Jesus Christ the Great High Priest.

The truth is that many of us, and many nations as well, have presumed that earthly strength affords us heavenly protection. It doesn't. King Uzziah presumed that he was above God's law, so he tried to do things *his way*, thinking, *God doesn't really mean what He says. He will make an exception for me. After all, I am the king of Judah, a ruler of this kingdom for half a century.*

All he got for his trouble was incurable leprosy, lifetime banishment from Judah's society, exile from the house of God and the palace of kings, and the curse of living the rest of his earthly life in sorrow and misery. Never let presumption pre-empt your purpose.

It is possible that had Uzziah rejected presumption and cho-sen humility, he could have become Judah's greatest king. Presumption preempted Uzziah's purpose and diverted his divine destiny. As it is, Judah's King Uzziah will forever be remembered as the king who started well, but finished in unspeakable sorrow.

In the end, it is likely that Uzziah's body was prepared for burial by other lepers. His own family members—including Isaiah the prophet—were forbidden to touch his leprous body.

What a sad end to such a fine beginning. And what a strong warning to us: Presumption is a dead-end street.

CHAPTER 8

A TALE OF TWO
KINGS AND A VEIL
*(Royal Robes of Pride or Humble
Coverings of Repentance)*

You don't have to experience tragedy to experience intimacy with God, but many of us seem to wait for crisis to rock our lives before we "lower ourselves" to run to the Rock of our Salvation.

When all hell broke loose over Manhattan's skyline on September 11, 2001, millions of people around the world dropped all pretense of political correctness and prayed, totally forgetting their carefully creased slacks, their immaculate business suits, or their dignified surroundings. Men and women in offices, homes, and manufacturing plants around America gathered to shamelessly bow their knees before the God of heaven and cry out for divine help.

Thousands of New Yorkers, renowned for their resilience and hardness to life's inconveniences, wept and prayed openly in the ashes of the World Trade Center while television cameras beamed the sight around the globe. It seems we all bend after tragedy and before we come to Him.

Perhaps I can't state this on a theological basis, but I will say on a philosophical one that even King Uzziah would have had to lay down the trappings of royalty and take up the simplicity of priesthood before he could rightly assume the duties and privileges of that sacred office.

You can't be insubordinate and submitted at the same time. There could be only one high king in the house of God—either Uzziah or the King of glory. According to the spiritual protocol established by the one true King through Moses under the Old Covenant, no one was to minister to the Lord at the veil except descendants of Aaron who had submitted to the ordinances of the priesthood. Yet David the shepherd-king managed to sit before the ark of God in the atmosphere created by his whole-hearted worship even though he was neither a descendent of Aaron nor a Levite. Isaiah the prophet—in the midst of his humility, weakness, and total dependence upon God after the funeral of Uzziah—was also able to see the Lord "high and lifted up" though he was neither Old Covenant priest nor Levite.

WE STILL FOLLOW ONE OF THESE
TWO KINGS—WITH PREDICTABLE RESULTS

King Uzziah and his distant predecessor, King David, represent two radically different approaches to the throne of God. Those approaches are still visible in the earth today, and their consequences still affect the destinies of men and nations. We still follow the path of one or the other of these two kings into the house of God—with predictable results.

The biblical "protocol of the spirit" requires us to come to a high level of intimacy with Divinity if we ever want to see Him high and lifted up. Under the rigid guidelines of the Old Covenant, priests had to follow a strict physical regimen of cleansing and purification as well.

Unfortunately, nearly everybody wants shortcuts to encountering God. Jesus was looking for eternal relationship with mankind while the people were only looking for a right-now deliverer, a way to get enough free bread for the next meal, or yet one more miracle to gossip about at the street market.

King Uzziah basically was saying what many of us have said in our day: "I don't want to go through all that spiritual protocol. I don't want to wait for the priestly anointing. Frankly, I don't want to go through the 'if My people' part of the promise either. I just want to go straight to the 'heal their land' part."[1]

Everyone seems to like talking about the Bible passage that says, "I will hear from heaven, and will forgive their sin and heal their land." Hardly anyone talks about the part that comes before it, the passage that says, "I . . . have chosen this place for Myself as a house of sacrifice."[2]

FEW ARE WILLING TO PURSUE HIM
WITHOUT REGARD TO POSITION OR PLACE

We like to rush through that part, but before the land is healed, we must build a house of sacrifice. Everyone wants God to choose his or her house, children, church, and nation, but few are willing to choose God and pursue Him with all of their hearts without regard to position or place.

We want God to choose *this* place. We want God to choose *this* church. We want *this* to be a place of revival. We want *this* to be a place of outreach. There is one small hitch to becoming "God's choice." If His finger does point you out, the first thing He is going to do is sacrifice you. "I have chosen this place for Myself *as a house of sacrifice*." Jesus said, "If anyone desires to come after Me, let him deny himself, and take up his cross daily, and follow Me. For whoever desires to save his life will lose it, but whoever loses his life for My sake will save it."[3]

"Yeah, but I don't like that part. I want to get straight to the good stuff, the healing of the land part." There is no shortcut to revival or restoration.

Too many Christians want to do things King Uzziah's way; they want "microwave revival." We want it push-button, with no muss, no fuss, and no commitment. In fact, most of us try to "import" prepackaged revival and renewal into our churches and cities.

REVIVAL AND RESTORATION
MUST BE BIRTHED AT OUR OWN ALTARS

You cannot import revival. The days of importing the right preacher and of programming just the right song are over. If we want to see revival, it will have to be birthed at our altars.

There isn't a preacher on the planet who qualifies as your Source. If you want the Real Thing, He is waiting for you. But first you must take off one set of robes and put on another. With that in mind, this is how I would respond to Uzziah:

Be careful, Uzziah. You can't circumvent God's protocol. If you ever hope to go behind the veil, then there is a process you must follow. To be honest with you, Uzziah, I don't know if you will want to pay the price to go behind the veil.

If you really want to go beyond the veil separating you

from His holiness, then you must resign from your position as earthly king. There are crowned kings seated on thrones of power arranged before God's throne this moment who constantly fall down and cast their crowns before Him before offering priestly praise and worship to Him as the King of kings and the Most High God.[4]

You must renounce your kingship to announce your priesthood. There can be only one Lord in your life.

You must give up ruling in your realm with the strength of man if you want to rule in His realm in the strength of the Spirit.

Too many of us want to lean on our own strength, but He says, "Trust in the LORD with all your heart, and lean not on your own understanding."[5]

A season of crisis is the perfect time to transfer your trust from your earthly resources to your heavenly Source. We must come alive to the message of God's Word, "Some trust in chariots, and some in horses; but we will remember the name of the LORD our God."[6]

Uzziah, you say you want to go, but if you really want to have an intimate encounter with Divinity, then you must take off humanity's crown. You will need to strip off those royal robes because you cannot just slip the priestly ephod of God over the royal robes of men. You can't cling to the trappings of royalty and at the same time put on the trappings of the priesthood. You must choose one or the other. You must either lean on the strength of man or totally depend on God.

Remember, Mr. Uzziah, that the Levites, the members of the priestly tribe, have no inheritance among men. God Himself is their inheritance. Are you willing to put your total trust in your Source instead of your resources? If you are willing to do that, then you can enter the land of perfect peace and total trust. But there are no shortcuts to that place. In fact, if you try to take the shortcut, you are going to get burned.

King Uzziah offered arrogance, and he was forcibly removed from the house of God. King David offered brokenness, and he was brought into the most intimate place of fellowship with Divinity though he was neither an Aaronic priest nor a Levite.

Why was King David allowed to go behind the veil of separation when King Uzziah was not? It was because David danced before the ark of the covenant the day he led the procession to return it to Jerusalem—*and he began that dance by stripping off his royal robes.*

We know he was virtually naked because it embarrassed his wife, Michal.[7] All he wore was a priestly ephod or short tunic that would barely manage to cover him.

DON'T WORRY ABOUT THE SPECTATORS
IN THE BALCONIES OF RELIGION

There will always be spectators who look down from the balconies of religion to ridicule worshippers who strip themselves down to the bare necessities.

King David was Israel's greatest warrior, leader, and king. Yet he thought nothing of stripping away all of the trappings of man's strength so he could worship the Lord without hindrance or limitation. He decided, "I am going to be a worshiper, and I cannot worship in human arrogance. I must do more than take off my crown; I will strip away my royal robes and every vestige of my earthly office."

David's wife, Michal, accosted him over the supper table and said in disdain, "David, you made a fool of yourself today. You should have seen yourself spinning and dancing and whirling. Couldn't you see how foolish you looked? Some king you are!"[8]

I can see him as his face turns ashen and he realizes just how different his values are from those of his wife. She was the daughter of King Saul, Israel's first king, and the first king to die in office (but out of God's favor).

Then it dawns on him. I can almost hear his reply to Michal's scorn:

> "Michal, I know this king business means a lot to you, because your father was a king and now you are married to the king. But I'm going to tell you something—*long before I was a king, I was a worshiper*. You think I was acting foolish today, but you should have seen me on the backside of the pasture when there was nobody around but me and the sheep! Today, *I decided to come out of the closet and do in public what I have always done in private. If you think this was bad, I will be even more undignified than this!*"[9]

This is the hour for Christians to "come out of the closet" and do in the streets of our cities what they have finally begun to do in the aisles of their churches! This is the time for them to take their places in the streets worshiping God and serving man in the hour of crisis.[10]

If the religious critics and worldly pundits think this is bad, we will be even more undignified and less religious than this!

We will take off our royal robes any day if we can approach the holiness of His presence and lead the lost to His fold.

This is the tale of two kings and a veil: One approached God arrayed in robes of royalty and the other approached Divinity arrayed in humble coverings of repentance. Only one entered God's presence and received the reward of intimacy. Which robes will you choose in times of crisis or periods of peace?

CHAPTER 9

WHO IS WILLING TO BECOME A SIGNPOST OF SAFETY?

(Paying the Price to Preserve Divine Purpose and Human Potential)

It seems to me that throughout human history, God has gone to great lengths to plant courageous men and women in strategic times and places as "signposts" or warning signs of danger to each generation.

He had Noah warn his neighbors for many years before the flood covered the earth.[1] This was a classic case of where it could be said, "You were warned!"

God twice preserved Moses from premature death and spent eighty years preparing him to deliver the descendants of Jacob from Egyptian bondage. In the process, He sent Moses as His prophet to confront Pharaoh again and again with warnings *before* the plagues were unleashed on Egypt. Pharaoh *could have* submitted to the will of God and spared the land, the water, the harvest, the firstborn of Egypt, and the elite troops of Pharaoh's army. He didn't, and all of these were lost.

Throughout the Old Testament era, God sent prophets almost exclusively to be living "Danger Ahead" and "Go This Way" signs for kings, governments, and nations. King David was one of the few kings who noticed and obeyed God's warning signs and preserved his life and potential (at least in part) through his obedience.

Fortunately for King David, God sent Nathan the prophet to confront the king over his adultery with Bathsheba and the premeditated murder of her husband. David obeyed this divine stop sign, repented of his sin, and continued to serve God. (He still paid a terrible price, including the death of his firstborn son and the fatal rebellion of another son, Absalom.[2])

STAY OFF THE GRASS OF HOLINESS!

In the case of King Uzziah, God planted eighty-one human warning signs in front of Judah's headstrong king in a last-ditch effort to divert him from his most costly crisis. Despite the efforts of eighty-one priests to shout, "Keep off the grass of holiness!" King Uzziah tried to forge ahead where angels fear to tread unasked. He ignored God's warning signs and reaped tragic consequences.

But when [King Uzziah] *was strong his heart was lifted up, to his destruction, for he transgressed against the LORD his God by entering the temple of the LORD to burn incense on the altar of incense. So Azariah the priest went in after him, and with him were eighty priests of the LORD, who were valiant men. And they withstood King Uzziah, and said to him, "It is not for you, Uzziah, to burn incense to the LORD, but for the priests, the sons of Aaron, who are consecrated to burn incense. Get out of the sanctuary, for you have trespassed! You shall have no honor from the LORD God."*[3]

King Uzziah had developed a serious problem with assumption, presumption, and arrogance by this point in his reign. Any one of those problems can prove fatal, but he managed to operate in all three of them. God sent the high priest with eighty other courageous priests to stand between Uzziah and the veil of the Holy of Holies. Frankly, those priests weren't there to protect God; they were there to preserve Uzziah from instant death.

KINGLY STRENGTH IS NOT EQUAL TO GODLY OMNIPOTENCE

The priests took their stand between the arrogant king who had the power to order their execution and the altar of the One who gave them life. Had God not shown up, those men could have lost their jobs and their heads, but they stood their ground. I can almost hear their urgent warnings: "Don't go there! Don't do that! Uzziah, you are making a mistake. God's glory is dangerous. God is jealous. Uzziah, do not assume that kingly strength is equal to godly omnipotence. You are strong, Uzziah. Sure, you tore down the gates of Gath and did some great things. But, Uzziah, don't go *there*."

Equally valiant servants of God have thundered across the pulpits of Christendom and taken their stand week after week, saying, "Don't go there; you are treading on dangerous ground! If you want to go there, you will have to change something about the way you do things."

We need valiant ministers with enough courage and faith to stand against the secular tide when destiny demands it. Secular thinking has increasingly dominated the business, educational, and governmental sectors of American life. The truth is that the secular realm has been guilty of spiritual trespass.

WE ARE NOT SELF-SUFFICIENT; WE ARE GOD-DEFICIENT

If we have learned anything through the tragedy of the terrorist attacks on September 11, 2001, it should be this: We are not *self-sufficient;* we are *God-deficient.* Our future depends on our ability to resist the subtle seduction of leaning on our own strength. We are weak apart from the strength of His grace.

An amazing tale of divine provision during the attack on the World Trade Center towers came across my desk recently. It illustrates the weakness of man's security and the power of God's provision. According to the e-mail report from a Christian organization via a former press correspondent living in New York, one man was injured by shattered glass in the initial attack on the first tower. He had been told to wait in the building's underground lobby where he would be safe, but he sensed strongly that he should go outside.

Just before he left the lobby the man said, "I'm leaving. Is anyone coming with me?" Then he opened the door and plunged into complete darkness. The people who had followed him called out in alarm, and he told them to follow his voice.

As everyone called out the name of Jesus, he noticed a trail of water and a slight current of fresh air in the darkness. He crawled and walked down a dark corridor following the wind current until he came to an opening. Then he led the small group of survivors out of the building toward the dim light of the ash-obscured sun just seconds before the building collapsed.

NEVER DEPEND ON THE SECURITY OF MAN

It wasn't until he made it back to the relative safety of his home that the man realized that the Lord had revealed two significant truths that day. First, we should never depend on the security man has built, and second, we must be led by the wind of God and the water because they direct us to the Son.[4]

Many in secular circles grow impatient with what is perceived as the "old way of thinking" about such spiritual and moral questions as public prayer and the innate value of life at conception and its cessation. (Some would use proabortion laws to grasp at the power to selectively decide who is born; others advocate euthanasia laws to decide who must die early.)

In nearly every case, the goal of shaking off old religious ideas is achieved by eroding or destroying the sacred relationship and exclusive privileges between parent and child. These secular social and spiritual engineers wish to cast aside the spiritual protocol laid down in God's Word and engineer things into a brave new world of their own making—one wholly separate from the spiritual. What a grim world that would be. . . .

Sometimes warning signs work. People listen, change their ways, and live to enjoy other days. Much of the time the warnings are ignored. Twice in one conversation, Jesus warned the judgmental critics of His day, ". . . unless you repent you will all likewise perish."[5]

King Uzziah's response to divine signposts is generally typical of the human race. Whenever someone dared to say, "It's time to repent," he became angry and upset. Earthly kings tend to get angry, go to war, and tear down any competing towers.

Uzziah forgot that in the presence of God there is only one King and that all human titles disappear. He wasn't dealing with merely eighty-one men or employees who worked in the temple; he had come face to face with eighty-one divinely ordained signposts separating him from the wrath of a jealous God.

WHEN KINGS GET ANGRY, TOWERS FALL; WHEN GOD GETS ANGRY, KINGS FALL

We must learn to understand the difference between the anger of mere men and the danger zone of God. Despite the clear warning, "Get out of the sanctuary, for you have trespassed!" Uzziah continued to approach the holy presence of God with a container of incense and a heart of rebellion. Disaster was only one step away, and the earthly king took the step that permanently diverted his destiny.

Then Uzziah became furious; and he had a censer in his hand to burn incense. And while he was angry with the priests, leprosy broke out on his forehead, before the priests in the house of the LORD, beside the incense altar. And Azariah the chief priest and all the priests looked at him, and there, on his forehead, he was leprous; so they thrust him out of that place. Indeed he also hurried to get out, because the LORD had struck him.[6]

Uzziah's assumption that his title in the earthly realm entitled him to authority in the spiritual realm led to presumption in both realms. Finally, his presumption led him beyond the boundary of grace and into divine judgment.

King Uzziah pushed past God's warning signs in presumptive arrogance until he heard eighty-one men suddenly take in their breath in shock and dismay. They had seen a spot of leprosy appear on the king's forehead. The king said, "What's wrong?" Perhaps someone brought him a mirror to reflect his own image of uncleanness. He had arrogantly trespassed into God's realm while clothed in sin, and it cost him all of the trappings of earthly royalty, authority, and acceptance.

The sad end of the story is that King Uzziah lived for many more years, but he wasn't really alive. "King Uzziah was a leper until the day of his death. He dwelt in an isolated house, because he was a leper; for he was cut off from the house of the LORD . . . ."[7]

HUMAN ARROGANCE DISQUALIFIES
US FROM DIVINE PRESENCE

This king's arrogance had disqualified him from entering God's house and abiding in His presence. It didn't matter who he was; time and chance come to every man along with tragedy and crisis.[8] He discovered that hot tears can soak the silk pillows of the wealthy and powerful as well as the paltry pillows of the poor and the weak. Everybody—even kings, dictators, and presidents—are subject to tragedy.

From then on Uzziah was king in name only. He existed, but he did not enjoy life. His son had to rule as a regent in his place, and he was essentially confined to house arrest in a communal house of lepers.

He owned the palace, but he couldn't live in it. Uzziah had the authority of a king, but he couldn't exercise it. Thirty seconds of spiritual trespass demoted this mighty earthly king to life as a bitter spiritual outcast. In the end, one of Judah's greatest "good" kings died alone, remembered only as the leper king—the man who trespassed against God and was judged.

Millions stand in the valley of decision. Who is willing to become an anointed signpost of safety in the hand of God? Who is willing to lovingly pay the price to preserve divine purpose and human potential—even if it puts him or her at risk from the anger of men?

CHAPTER 10

WHERE DO YOU GO AFTER YOU COME HOME FROM A FUNERAL?
(You Must Depose the Old King to Discover the Real King)

Where do you go when you're feeling weak at the knees and your source of strength has dried up? This is not a good time to run *from* the Lord; this is the time you should run *to* the Lord.

It has been reported to me that on the Sunday following the terrorist attacks on September 11, 2001, America's churches noted perhaps the largest attendance in the past few years. People were crowding into church buildings everywhere. The number of people attending services in some places was even larger than at Christmas or Easter. Buried somewhere in the instinctual emotions of man, there is a drive in the soul that cries, "I have to find God." Trust comes easier after a tragedy.

Pass by the church after the funeral; that's the one place you need to go when the weight of life and crisis becomes too heavy to bear. Times of crisis are opportune times for us to invite other people to the presence of God as well. People in pain are often just looking for directions to run to the High Tower. Why don't you call? Why don't you tell those in the midst of tragedy, "You know, this would be a good time to go to God."

Consider where Isaiah went after crisis visited his life. There is no better time to go to church than when you are coming home from a funeral. Why? Because very often it's only after the false king in your life has died that the true king can be crowned.

The only cure for the Uzziah Syndrome is an Isaiah experience with God that you will never get over. Most of us never make it to that point because we get angry when we are confronted with the truth. We get angry instead of yielding to sorrowful repentance, and we insist on swinging our sacred religious censors filled with unauthorized and unacceptable offerings. What we need are burning lips and a hot heart. One coal from His altar will cure our arrogance.[1]

How many times had Isaiah been in the temple? We are sure he was a frequent visitor there, but perhaps he also was one of those who spoke in the courtyard. After all, Isaiah was already considered to be an eloquent and prophetic voice to his generation (even *before* his encounter with the Lord "high and lifted up").

HOW OFTEN HAD HE GONE TO CHURCH IN CALMER TIMES?

How many times had the prophet been to church and satisfied his soul with the religious process of going through the program, punching the buttons, and focusing on the familiar patterns of merely human endeavor? How often had he gone to church in calmer times and been satisfied by the unmoving patterns on the veil of separation, the monotone citation of the priests, and the fragrant smoke of the incense?

Did Isaiah have any hint of the divine potential waiting just beyond the veil for those whose desperation brought them face to face with the Lord, high and lifted up?

It is more than coincidental that Isaiah retreated to the temple after King Uzziah's death. As a prophet, we may assume Isaiah had been to the temple many times. The day came, however, during a time of crisis, when Isaiah entered the doors of the temple with a different attitude.

AFTER THE FUNERAL, ISAIAH
WAS DESPERATE FOR GOD

After the funeral, Isaiah didn't go to the temple for the smoke of the incense and sacrifice. He wasn't anticipating the sound of the tinkling bells on priestly robes; he wasn't interested in gazing at the veil of separation. Isaiah came because he was desperate for God.

Desperation is often the birth child of crisis. This man's earthly king and political mentor had just died. Isaiah's royal cousin and constant companion was finally gone after a humiliating and lingering finish as the leper king who dared to presume upon the holiness of God.

The wisest thing you can do personally is to take advantage of your own tenderness in the aftermath of crisis and tragedy. Like a child running to a parent, turn to Him who is the Source of all strength and allow Him to draw you to Himself. Allow Him to stretch out and extend your moments of intimacy as Father and child. You also will find that in times of tragedy, those around you will be tender. Be sensitive to their tenderness even in your own grief and pain. The wisest thing you can do for them, while they are tender, is tell them who they can trust.

I still remember how I felt when I realized that what I was experiencing had all of the characteristics of grief. Somebody or something had died, and I was traveling the humanly familiar roads in a difficult journey back to some measure of normalcy.

Grief carries us past several measuring points, which may include denial and isolation, anger, bargaining, and even depression before we finally accept the reality of separation and loss.

THIS ISN'T A MOVIE

When I observed the calamity that engulfed the World Trade Center towers and the Pentagon, my first words were, "This can't be happening. This isn't real. This is what you see in the movies" . . . but this wasn't a movie. Then the journey from tragedy to trust and triumph had to be started and completed— one trudging step at a time.

What made me think along these lines? It happened when I compared the yardstick of my emotions with the level of the tragedy around me. I felt as if I had just come home from a funeral of someone I know.

The grief of the nation became more personal, came even closer to home, again that same day. Shortly after the tragedy began to unfold, I was talking on the phone with one of my faithful and valued assistants about normal and routine ministry matters. I had hardly hung up the phone when a sudden page came across our office phone system asking everyone to pray for my assistants brother, who was in the World Trade Center complex. *How could that be?* I thought. *I just hung up the phone with her.* I learned later that she had received notification just after I hung up the phone.

In that brief moment I learned that tragedy was no longer six degrees separated from me—it had moved into my own life to affect those I loved and worked with each day.

I quickly redialed my assistant, but this time my call was anything but "business as usual." Time seemed to stop for all of us at GodChaser.network until my assistant finally heard from her brother—bruised and battered, but alive.

DISINTERESTED BYSTANDERS
NEED NOT APPLY

Something else happened in that moment as well. Suddenly the approximately six thousand people lost or counted as missing from the World Trade Center towers, the Pentagon attack, and the four hijacked airliners became more than nameless faces. I was mourning the tragic deaths of people I didn't even know, and I was also mourning the loss of something far greater. It wasn't just reading anonymous obituaries any longer.

When a Christian sees someone fall into a "gorilla pit," he or she doesn't have the option of being a disinterested bystander. The Christian who reacts with tenderness in times of tragedy will be remembered with gratitude when good times come again.

Our response to tragedy as individuals and as a body of believers, whether the crisis strikes a neighbor, our community, or our nation, may set up the success or failure of the church in the days ahead.

When embroiled in the high emotional content of a crisis, remember there is no better time to act than *now*. Take courage, speak up, but speak tenderly and serve with compassion.

Remember that God has *always* been there; it is our attitudes that changed on the way home from a funeral. Too many of us go to church with one attitude, seeing only one thing.

DEPENDENCY LETS YOU LOOK
PAST THE SMOKE

Things look different when we go to church after a funeral. The weight of our grief and sorrow over precious loved ones and life dreams lost often produces an attitude of brokenness and repentance. This causes at least two very important things to happen. First, this kind of attitude allows us to see past the pastor's preaching and peer beyond the singing of the choir or worship team. Dependency lets us look past the smoke of the burning incense to see the throne where the Lord awaits us high and lifted up.

The second thing that happens is described in my book, *The God Catchers*:

> Sometimes you come in your fullness and make yourself empty, as Zacchaeus did. At other times you cry out in your bankruptcy, hunger, and pain, and God shows up. That's the cry God can't deny. David the psalmist knew about the key of genuine brokenhearted desperation. He vividly described it for anyone who wanted to see it:
>
> For You do not desire sacrifice, or else I would give it;
> You do not delight in burnt offering.
> The sacrifices of God are *a broken spirit,*
> *A broken and a contrite heart—*
> *These, O God, You will not despise.*[2]

There is no better time to have an encounter with God than when you are going home from a funeral. When I read Isaiah's account of his encounter with God in the temple in Isaiah 6, it almost seems as if God set him up for a personal and private meeting.

I can almost hear Him say, "I have been waiting on you,

Isaiah. I have been waiting for you to depose the *other* king in your life. Now that the earthly king has been removed from the throne of your life, I have decided to show you what the real King is like. You thought the glory of the other king was incredible, but wait until you see *My* glory."

CHAPTER 11

WILL YOU BE WAITING AFTER THE FUNERAL?
(Becoming God's Lighthouse of Compassion in the Storm of Crisis)

If you saw that young boy fall into the gorilla enclosure we mentioned earlier, how appropriate would it be for you to walk away wagging your head saying, "It was *his* fault! He should have known better"?

In the same way, you and I have a responsibility to intervene and intercede on behalf of the hurting and those in crisis. God wants us to permanently retire our judges' robes and self-righteous tones. Without exception, we are sinners saved by grace.[1]

My mind recoils at the scene of the hapless young boy lying unconscious and immobile in imminent danger. He could do nothing to help himself; it was up to others to save him. The truth is that no matter how strong, intelligent, or wealthy you may be, you too could easily reach a point at which you are too weak to defend or save yourself.

Although some tragedies could be prevented or avoided by right decisions and actions, it is still not our place to judge others when their failures or mistakes land them in a crisis. We have a biblical mandate to intervene and intercede for others in need as God's divine paramedics. This is God's idea of right attitudes and right actions:

> *Is this not the fast that I have chosen: To loose the bonds of wickedness, to undo the heavy burdens, to let the oppressed go free, and that you break every yoke? Is it not to share your bread with the hungry, and that you bring to your house the poor who are cast out; when you see the naked, that you cover him, and not hide yourself from your own flesh? . . . If you take away the yoke from your midst, the pointing of the finger, and speaking wickedness, if you extend your soul to the hungry and satisfy the afflicted soul, then your light shall dawn in the darkness, and your darkness shall be as the noonday.*[2]

BECOME A LIGHTHOUSE IN THE STORM

Isaiah became a living tower of hope and guidance after his encounter with God. Like a lighthouse in a storm, he steered his nation clear of the rocks of pride, presumption, and prejudice. Isaiah faithfully warned, encouraged, and comforted a nation held captive in a time of crisis. He became a man energized with the power and authority of God.

Unfortunately, this kind of man seems to be in short supply right now. Perhaps that explains why so many people pass by Christianity so often.

What would Jesus do in our situation? We know that He wept at the tomb of Lazarus.[3] Perhaps you can't speak the words of resurrection life with the authority Jesus did when He raised Lazarus from the grave, but surely you can weep with the same passion Jesus had when He cried at the death of a friend.

I have a feeling that if we do what we can do as mere humans, then God will step in and do what only Divinity can do. Are you at a loss over what to do for your hurting neighbor or wounded boss? Take a cue from Jesus, who said, "Blessed are those who mourn, for they shall be comforted,"[4] and the writer of Romans who said, "Rejoice with those who rejoice, and weep with those who weep."[5]

THEY NEED EXTRICATION FROM DARKNESS

Mark and Betsy Neuenschwander, a husband and wife physician team, wrote in their book, *Crisis Evangelism: Preparing to Be Salt and Light When the World Needs Us Most*:

It seems prudent for us to take our cues from Christ and become poised to utilize tragic events to maximize His deepest desire: that none should perish but all come to the knowledge of Him (2 Pet. 3:9). If we fail to do so, what will be our excuses? Is it that we are too busy with jobs, families, kids and church activities, with no time or money left over to undertake Christian disaster evangelism? Also, we assume that the National Guard, FEMA or Civil Defense personnel will do it, right? But as helpful as these agencies are, they do not offer rescue from the greatest disaster of the universe—eternity in hell. *People often come to Christ in crisis because their shallow, false foundations are in rubble. They need extrication from the kingdom of darkness into the Kingdom of light!*[6]

We can't tell the good news and be the bad news of an uncaring attitude!

Crisis seems to burn into our memories the crucial dates, smells, surroundings, and visual cues marking its passage. I can still remember the exact place I was standing—on the back porch steps of the house at 114 Slack Street in West Monroe, Louisiana—when the reality of President John F. Kennedy's assassination hit me. I was in the second grade.

If every generation has its hallmark tragedy and a date "that will live in infamy," then perhaps every home and every individual will be tested in the private crucible of his or her own crisis or tragedy.

America was not the same after the December 7 attack on Pearl Harbor. Neither did our nation immediately return to normal after the assassination of President Kennedy. We became stronger, more united, and more cohesive for a time—and more aware of the frailty of life.

Tragedy will either tear you apart or glue you together. We often have no control over the tragedy that comes into our lives. However, we always have control over our reaction to life's circumstances—whether we're blessed and abounding or bleeding and wounded. You can't control the tragedy factor, but you can control the trust factor!

May we persevere with the same attitude as Job and encourage ourselves and others with his words birthed in a time of incredible crisis: "Naked I came from my mother's womb, and naked shall I return there. The LORD gave, and the LORD has taken away; blessed be the name of the LORD."[7] Job also said, "Though *He* slay me [much less a terrorist or a tragedy], yet will I trust Him."[8] Trust is built by a history of reliability, not the crisis of the moment. Comfort yourself by understanding that if God fails you, you will be the first person in history whom He's ever failed.

YOUR RESPONSE TO CRISIS
MAY DETERMINE YOUR FUTURE

A Christian's response to crisis and tragedy in his own life and in the lives of those around him often determines whether he or she gets stronger or weaker. Your response to crisis may determine your future.

Perhaps future generations will one day speak of the tragedy of September 11, 2001, with the same benign absence of emotion and empathy that we demonstrate when we say, "In the year that king Uzziah died. . . ." I hope not. Our sense of invincibility vanished the day simple box cutters wielded by suicidal terrorists brought down millions of tons of concrete and steel in two of America's tallest buildings. My personal hope is that we remember how this crisis took the wind out of America's sails of invincibility and replaced them with the calm breeze of humility.

WHAT ARE YOUR WEAPONS OF RESPONSE?

The right word spoken at the right moment, the right prayer prayed at the right time, the right song sung at the right service, the right balm applied at the point of pain—these should be our weapons of response in times of crisis.

The simple weapons of worship in the hands of compassion and love can cause the walls of Jericho to fall in Satan's kingdom. Isaiah went into the temple and worshiped when suddenly a fresh vision of the real King filled the room—and he was never the same. Normal would no longer do for him. He had seen the King of kings.

More than five thousand people from America and many other nations lost their lives in the vicious terrorist attack on September 11, 2001, and we mourn their tragic deaths. Yet something else died that day as well, and this was one death that was long overdue: America's arrogance died that September morning. I pray it will not return. Humility will serve us far better and preserve us far longer than arrogance. The aftermath of a tragedy is a fertile field for the rebirth of humility and dependence on God.

"Isaiah, where are you going?"

"I am coming home from a funeral. I am going to pass by the church."

Tragedy often passes by the church after the fact. When crisis grips a nation, a family, or an individual, we, the body of

Christ, have an opportunity to find our voices and speak comforting words from the heart of the Lord. The door of opportunity opens for Christian Marys and Marthas to bind up the brokenhearted, provide food and drink, and meet their every need in an atmosphere of unconditional love marked by worship and adoration to the true King.[9]

When you gather around the coffeepot in your office this week or meet coworkers for a lunch break, realize you may be walking into a divine appointment. This is your chance to say, "What do you think?" When they talk *tragedy*, it's your chance to talk *trust*.

Revival can start with the match of a terrorist just as easily as with a match from a revivalist, but circumstances alone cannot bring revival to pass. It takes the marriage of human desperation to divine passion and presence.

IMAGINE WALL STREET BUSINESSES JAMMED WITH PRAYING MEN

In 1865, a man named Jeremiah Lampier started a prayer meeting with fourteen people in a belfry tower of the North Dutch Reformed Church just one block off of Wall Street in New York City. The following week twenty-eight people showed up. The prayer revival swept through the community until every church on Wall Street was jammed with praying men at the noon lunch hour.

In February of that year, the Baptists were baptizing ten thousand converts a week (even though they had to cut holes in the ice covering the Hudson River to conduct the baptisms).

Horace Greeley, the owner and publisher of *The New York Herald Tribune*, asked a reporter to find out how many people were praying on Wall Street that day. Since the reporter was limited to a horse and buggy for transportation, he could only go to six prayer sites before press time. He still counted 6,000 men spending their lunch hour in prayer! A *crisis* precipitated that revival—Wall Street had suffered a severe stock market crash that year that drove people to their knees in prayer.

There is no more opportune time to pray or to be available to pray with others than after a crisis. Sometimes we almost feel invincible in our arrogance, as if destiny may never have a day with us. Yet the rain falls on the just as well as on the unjust.[10]

It seems that at times the only way out of the valley of the shadow of death is to forge right through it. I read where one lady said, "The only way out is through." Perhaps you can't "unspill" the milk or undo the damage done in the past, but you *can* apply a bandage and move closer to the Creator of all.

If you personally feel yourself to be at a time of crisis, there is no better time than now to learn to trust the Lord. If someone around you has just suffered a tragedy, gently lead that person to trust. As the song says, "'Tis so sweet to trust in Jesus"! Pray this prayer with me now:

Dear Father, there is a river of tears flowing, brought on by catastrophe and crisis. It flows from individual broken hearts and from entire families living in the shadow of despair. It floods the landscape of entire nations and cultures, and yet there is a great Hope among us.

We come to You, Father, because we want to repent of our arrogance. We repent of that spirit of invincibility and pride that led us to lean on the arm of mere men and women.

Lord, we also repent of falsely attributing our prosperity to our own ingenuity. We watched two powerful towers fall under the hatred of a handful of evil men. Our financial strength and our military might were smitten. Now we cry out, "What are we going to do?"

Lord, we discovered something wonderful in the midst of our pain and sorrow. When men and circumstances struck at the very heart of our strength, we suddenly discovered that the name of the Lord is a strong tower and the righteous run to it and are safe. We call on Your name right now. We acknowledge Jesus as our only Savior.

So we say, "Lord, have mercy. Have mercy on us and on our nation. Have mercy on us as a people, and have mercy upon me." As Your body, Lord, we repent and intercede for those who are incapable of helping themselves. We stand in the gap on their behalf and cry out . . .

O Lord, You are our Shelter and High Tower; our ever present Help in time of need. Forgive us, cleanse us, deliver us, and comfort us, Lord. We love and worship You. In Jesus' name we pray, amen.

If you prayed this prayer, please contact me. I want to be able to encourage you. Write, call, or e-mail: Tommy Tenney, Godchasers.network, P.O. Box 3355, Pineville, LA 71361, (318) 442-4273, www.godchasers.net.

NOTES

CHAPTER 1

1. See Luke 13:1–5.
2. Luke 13:1–3 NIV, emphasis mine.
3. Luke 13:4 NLT.
4. Whether Pilate diverted some sacred Jewish funds to construct an aqueduct from the pool of Siloam, or a tower in the city wall fell into the ancient pool, we do not know. We do know the Jews were angry about it. The Jewish historian, Josephus, a non-Christian contemporary of Jesus, apparently mentions the accident in his writings, according to Samuel J. Andrews. Andrews wrote in his book, *The Life of Our Lord Upon the Earth* (New York: Charles Scribner's Sons, 1891), 395: "Of the tower that fell in Siloam we have no knowledge, but as Josephus (War, v. 4. 3) speaks of the towers in the city walls, it has been conjectured that it was one of them. It is said by some, as Pressense, that it occurred during the building of the aqueduct by Pilate."

CHAPTER 2

1. Isaiah 6:1, emphasis mine.
2. Tommy Tenney, *The God Catchers* (Nashville: Thomas Nelson Publishers, 2000), 15–16, emphasis mine.
3. Department of Defense. 50th Anniversary of World War II Commemorative Committee. *Pearl Harbor: 50th Anniversary Commemorative Chronicle, "A Grateful Nation Remembers" 1941–1991.*

Washington: The Committee, 1991. Naval Historical Center, FAQ #105, "The Pearl Harbor Attack, 7 December 1941." 2 October 2001. 22 October 2001 <http://www.history.navy.mil/faqs/faq66-1.htm>.

4. Matthew 5:4.

5. Psalm 34:18a.

6. God said, ". . . My gracious favor is all you need. My power works best in your weakness" (2 Corinthians 12:9a NLT).

7. See Proverbs 18:10.

CHAPTER 3

1. Luke 13:2–5 NLT.

2. John 3:16–17 NIV.

3. The first portion of this sentence is a paraphrase of Ecclesiastes 3:1.

4. 2 Chronicles 7:14.

5. I am not making this up. Jesus said, "The truth is, anyone who believes in me will do the same works I have done, and even greater works, because I am going to be with the Father. You can ask for anything in my name, and I will do it, because the work of the Son brings glory to the Father" (John 14:12–13 NLT). He also said in His final prayer in the garden of Gethsemane that He was sending us into the world just as His Father had sent Him (see John 17:18).

6. Isaiah 50:4 NLT, emphasis mine.

7. John 3:17 NIV.

8. Esther 4:14b.

CHAPTER 4

1. See Job 1–2; Zechariah 3:1; and Revelation 12:10, where Satan is referred to as an accuser.

2. Job 2:10b.

3. Job 13:15a, emphasis and bracketed insertion mine.

4. Matthew 5:44–45 NIV.

5. See Job 1:21–22.

6. 2 Chronicles 20:12 NIV, emphasis mine.

7. 2 Timothy 3:12 NIV.

8. See Proverbs 13:12.

9. John 14:6.

10. God has already "commissioned" us formally, but sometimes He must remind us. Jesus Christ delivered our original commission, often remembered as "the great commission," just before His ascension: "Then Jesus came to them and said, 'All authority in heaven and on earth has been given to me. Therefore go and make disciples of all nations, baptizing them in the name of the Father and of the Son and of the Holy Spirit, and teaching them to obey everything I have commanded you. And surely I am with you always, to the very end of the age'" (Matthew 28:18-20 NIV).

11. Matthew 11:28–29 NIV.

12. Tommy Tenney, *Chasing God, Serving Man: Divine Encounters Between Martha's Kitchen and Mary's Worship* (Shippensburg, Pa.: Fresh Bread, an imprint of Destiny Image Publishers, 2001), 126–127.

13. See John 14:6.

CHAPTER 5

1. See Acts 14:12–15.

2. Romans 8:26 NIV.

3. See Acts 9:1–9.

4. Tommy Tenney, *The God Catchers* (Nashville: Thomas Nelson Publishers, 2000), 71.

5. Ibid, 23.

6. Dan Van Veen, "Surviving the 81st Floor of World Trade Tower Two," Assemblies of God News Service, September 14, 2001, A/G News #601, 22 October 2001. <http://ag.org/top/index.cfm>.

7. Tenney, *The God Catchers*, 25.

CHAPTER 6

1. Job 1:21–22 NIV.

2. Isaiah 6:1.

3. See 2 Chronicles 26.

4. Psalm 122:6a.

5. 2 Chronicles 26:15.

6. 2 Chronicles 26:5b, emphasis mine.

7. Mark 12:30–31 NIV, emphasis mine.

8. Jeremiah 17:9–10 NIV.

9. Psalm 119:105 NIV.

10. Proverbs 18:10 NIV.

Chapter 7

1. 2 Chronicles 26:15b–16, emphasis mine.

2. 2 Chronicles 26:16b, emphasis mine.

CHAPTER 8

1. See 2 Chronicles 7:14.

2. 2 Chronicles 7:12b.

3. Luke 9:23–24.

4. See the scene depicted in Revelation 4:4,10.

5. Proverbs 3:5.

6. Psalm 20:7.

7. See 2 Samuel 6:14–20.

8. See 2 Samuel 6:20 in particular.

9. See 2 Samuel 6:21–22. Quoted from Tommy Tenney's sermon, "Going Home from a Funeral," available free from GodChasers.network at www.godchasers.net or (318) 442-4273.

10. For more information on the unique power released through Christians who know how to chase God and serve man at the same time, see my

book, *Chasing God, Serving Man: Divine Encounters Between Martha's Kitchen and Mary's Worship* (Shippensburg, Pa.: Fresh Bread, an imprint of Destiny Image Publishers, Inc., 2001).

Chapter 9

1. See Genesis 6 and 7.
2. See 2 Samuel 12:1–25.
3. 2 Chronicles 26:16–18.
4. Adapted from an article by Nicole Schiavi, "Man Was Led Through Darkness to Safety By the Wind and Water," distributed to the ELIJAH LIST, an e-mail-based intercessory prayer network and nonprofit Christian ministry. The e-mail noted that Nicole Schiavi is a web developer in New York City and was formerly a journalist for the Associated Press and a New Hampshire newspaper.
5. Luke 13:3b.
6. 2 Chronicles 26:19-20.
7. 2 Chronicles 26:21.
8. See Ecclesiastes 9:11 NIV.

CHAPTER 10

1. Tommy Tenney, *The God Catchers* (Nashville: Thomas Nelson Publishers, 2000), 21.
2. Ibid, 149–150, emphasis added.

CHAPTER 11

1. See Ephesians 2:8–9.
2. Isaiah 58:6–7, 9b–10.
3. See John 11:35.
4. Matthew 5:4.
5. Romans 12:15.

6. Mark Neuenschwander, M.D., and Betsy Neuenschwander, M.D., *Crisis Evangelism: Preparing to be Salt and Light When the World Needs Us Most* (Ventura, Calif.: Regal Books, a division of Gospel Light, 1999), 103, emphasis mine.

7. Job 1:21.

8. Job 13:15a, emphasis mine.

9. If you would like more information about the unique role of Marys and Marthas in the church, in revival, and in times of crisis, I encourage you to get a copy of my book, *Chasing God, Serving Man: Divine Encounters Between Martha's Kitchen and Mary's Worship* (Shippensburg, Pa.: Fresh Bread, an imprint of Destiny Image Publishers, Inc., 2001).

10. See Matthew 5:45.

ABOUT THE AUTHOR

Tommy Tenney is the author of the bestselling series *The God Chasers, God's Favorite House,* and *The God Catchers.* Adding to that series now are *How to Be a God Chaser and a Kid Chaser,* coauthored with his mother, and *Chasing God, Serving Man,* a revelatory revisiting of the story of Mary and Martha. He is also the author of another series of books on unity that includes *God's Dream Team, Answering God's Prayer,* and *God's Secret to Greatness.*

Tommy spent ten years pastoring and has spent over twenty years in itinerant ministry, traveling to more than forty nations. He speaks in over 150 venues each year sharing his heart with many thousands. His two passions are *The Presence of God* and *Unity in the Body of Christ.* To help others pursue these twin passions he founded the GodChasers.network, a ministry organized to distribute his writing and speaking through various media. Tommy is a prolific author with more than one million books in print each year, and eight bestselling titles to date. His books have been translated into more than twenty-two languages.

Three generations of ministry in his family heritage have given Tommy a unique perspective on ministry. He has a gifting to lead hungry people into the presence of God. He and his wife Jeannie understand the value of intimacy with God and humility in serving God's people.

The Tenneys reside in Louisiana with their three daughters and two Yorkies.

Look for Tommy's new major release in February 2002

In *God's Eye View*, Tommy Tenney explores how worship lifts us up to see the trouble we face from God's perspective instead of being trapped in an earthly, time-bound viewpoint. The higher we go, the smaller our problems seem.

Worship doesn't really change our problems; it just minimizes their influence over us as we focus on God. He doesn't promise to remove all of our circumstances, but God does assure us that in His presence and from His perspective—we can see things as they really are and not how they appear to be.

Higher than a bird's eye view, higher than a man's eye view is God's eye view.

God's Eye View
ISBN 0-7852-6560-0
Look for this book at your local bookstore,
or by visiting the Web site www.ThomasNelson.com
or calling 1-800-441-0511.

Catch Him!

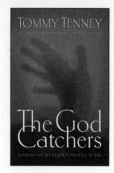 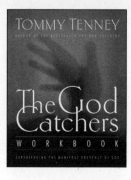 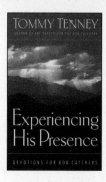

| *The God Catchers* | *The God Catchers Workbook* | *Experiencing His Presence* |
| ISBN 0-7852-6710-7 | ISBN 0-7852-6623-2 | ISBN 0-7852-6619-4 |

Why do some believers experience genuine, life-changing, personal revival while others don't? In *The God Catchers* and its companions, *The God Catchers Workbook* and the devotional *Experiencing His Presence,* Tommy explains the difference: "God in a sense plays hide and seek. But like a loving parent, He always makes sure He can be found by those who take the time to look." Simply put, those who earnestly seek God rather than wait for something to happen find Him. Full of biblical and contemporary accounts of believers who chased God and caught Him, these three books will motivate readers to discover the joy of finding God and having a loving relationship with Him.

Look for all of these books at your local bookstore,
or by visiting the Web site www.ThomasNelson.com
or calling 1-800-441-0511.

GOD*Chasers.network*

GodChasers.network is the ministry of Tommy and Jeannie Tenney. Their heart's desire is to see the presence and power of God fall—not just in churches, but on cities and communities all over the world.

How to contact us:

By Mail:

GodChasers.network
P.O. Box 3355
Pineville, Louisiana 71361
USA

By Phone:

Voice: 318.44CHASE (318.442.4273)
Fax: 318.442.6884
Orders: 888.433.3355

By Internet:

E-mail: GodChaser@GodChasers.net
Website: www.GodChasers.net

If you would like to obtain a free copy of the
audiotape message that inspired the book,

Trust and Tragedy

please contact us at 888.433.3355
or by mail at the address listed above.

Join Today

When you join the **GodChasers.network** we'll send you a free teaching tape!

If you share in our vision and want to stay current on how the Lord is using GodChasers.network, please add your name to our mailing list. We'd like to keep you updated on what the Spirit is saying through Tommy. We'll also send schedule updates and make you aware of new resources as they become available.

Sign up by calling or writing to:

Tommy Tenney
GodChasers.network
P.O. Box 3355
Pineville, Louisiana 71361-3355
USA

318-44CHASE (318.442.4273)
or sign up online at http://www.GodChasers.net/lists/

We regret that we are only able to send regular postal mailings to certain countries at this time. If you live outside the US you can still add your postal address to our mailing list—you will automatically begin to receive our mailings as soon as they are available in your area.

E-mail Announcement List

If you'd like to receive information from us via e-mail, just provide an e-mail address when you contact us and let us know that you want to be included on the e-mail announcement list!

BOOKS BY

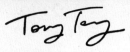

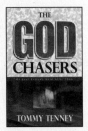

THE GOD CHASERS
$12.00 plus $4.50 S&H

What is a GodChaser? A person whose hunger exceeds his reach . . . a person who passion for God's presence presses him to chase the impossible in hopes that the uncatchable might catch him.

The great GodChasers of the scripture, Moses, Daniel, David... see how they where driven by hunger, born of tasting His goodness, they had seen the invisible and nothing else satisfied. Add your name to the list. Come join the ranks of the GodChasers.

CHASING GOD SERVING MAN
$17.00 plus $4.50 S&H

Using the backdrop of Bethany and the house of Mary and Martha, Tommy Tenney biblically explores new territory. The revolutionary concepts in this book can change your life. You will discover who you really are! (and unlock the secret of who "they" really are!)

THE GOD CATCHERS
$17.00 plus $4.50 S&H

Ever feel like you can't find God? Here's good news: God's not hiding from you, but for you. He wants you to know His loving presence in a way that only those who earnestly seek Him can. In his breakthrough bestseller *The God Chasers*, Tommy Tenney invited millions to the passionate pursuit of God. Now, in his long-anticipated sequel, *The God Catchers* explains how GodChasers can become "GodCatchers".

AUDIOTAPE ALBUMS BY

Tony Tenny

NEW!
WHAT'S THE FIGHT ABOUT?
(audiotape album) $20 plus $4.50 S&H

Tape 1 — Preserving the Family: God special gift to the world is the family! If we dont preserve the family, the church is one generation from extinction. Gods desire is to heal the wounds of the family from the inside out.

Tape 2 — Unity in the body: An examination of the levels of unity that must be respected and achieved before "Father let them be one" becomes an answered prayer!

Tape 3 — "IF you're throwing dirt, you're just loosing ground!" In "Whats the fight about?" Tommy invades our backyards to help us discover our differences are not so different after all!

FANNING THE FLAMES
(audiotape album) $20 plus $4.50 S&H

Tape 1 — The Application of the Blood and the Ark of the Covenant: Most of the churches in America today dwell in an outer-court experience. Jesus made atonement with His own blood, once for all, and the veil in the temple was rent from top to bottom.

Tape 2 — A Tale of Two Cities—Nazareth & Nineveh: What city is more likely to experience revival: Nazareth or Nineveh? You might be surprised....

Tape 3 — The "I" Factor: Examine the difference between *ikabod* and *kabod* ("glory"). The arm of flesh cannot achieve what needs to be done. God doesn't need us; we need Him.

KEYS TO LIVING THE REVIVED LIFE
(audiotape album) $20 plus $4.50 S&H

Tape 1 — Fear Not: To have no fear is to have faith, and that perfect love casts out fear, so we establish the trust of a child in our loving Father.

Tape 2 — Hanging in There: Have you ever been tempted to give up, quit, and throw in the towel? This message is a word of encouragement for you.

Tape 3 — Fire of God: Fire purges the sewer of our souls and destroys the hidden things that would cause disease. Learn the way out of a repetitive cycle of seasonal times of failure.

VIDEOTAPE ALBUMS BY

Tony Tenny

LET'S BUILD A BONFIRE VOL. 1: "LET IT FALL!"
Video $20.00 plus $4.50 S&H

Have you ever heard the warning, "Don't get too close to the fire, or you'll get burned?" If you get close enough to this fire, it will set you on fire and you'll never be the same! Our God is a consuming fire! (Heb 12:29) I want to be a Holy Ghost arsonist, setting fires of revival in the hearts of His people! That's exactly what we did in this GodChasers Gathering. This service burns with holy passion—and it can help you build a bonfire in your own life! This video features one hour of the best worship and word from the Tampa God Chaser gathering.

FOLLOW THE MAN ON THE COLT
Video $20.00 plus $4.50 S&H

From humility to authority…. If we learn to ride the colt of humility, then we qualify to ride on the stallion of authority.

This new video helps us understand that we all start this journey crawling—which strenghthens us to walk—that empowers us to run—and rewards us to ride! Enjoy this great teaching by Tommy Tenney on following the man on the colt. It will change the way you see the obstacles put in your path! Remember, there is never a testimony without a test!

BROWNSVILLE WILDFIRE SERIES, VOL. 1
"Born to Be a Worshipper"
Video $20.00 plus $4.50 S&H

God would rather hear the passionate praises of His children than the perfection of heavenly worship. It isn't about how good we are as singers, or how skilled we are as musicians. It isn't about singing catchy choruses with clever words. It's all about GOD, and if we'll let our guard down and allow ourselves to truly worship Him, we'll find that He's closer than we ever imagined.If you've been born into God's kingdom, then you were born to be a worshipper! It's time to do the very thing that we were created for!

Run With Us!

Become a GodChasers.network Monthly Revival Partner

Two men, a farmer and his friend, were looking out over the farmer's fields one afternoon. It was a beautiful sight—it was nearly harvest time, and the wheat was swaying gently in the wind. Inspired by this idyllic scene, the friend said, "Look at God's provision!" The farmer replied, "You should have seen it when God had it by Himself!"

This humorous story illustrates a serious truth. Every good and perfect gift comes from Him: but we are supposed to be more than just passive recipients of His grace and blessings. We must never forget that only God can cause a plant to grow—but it is equally important to remember that *we are called to do our part in the sowing, watering, and harvesting.*

When you sow seed into this ministry, you help us reach people and places you could never imagine. The faithful support of individuals like you allows us to send resources, free of charge, to many who would otherwise be unable to obtain them. Your gifts help us carry the Gospel all over the world—including countries that have been closed to evangelism. Would you prayerfully consider partnering with us? As a small token of our gratitude, our Revival Partners who send a monthly gift of $20 or more receive a teaching tape every month. This ministry could not survive without the faithful support of partners like you!

Stand with me now—so we can run together later!

In Pursuit,

Tommy Tenney

Tommy Tenney

**Become a Monthly Revival Partner by calling
or writing to and receive:**

Tommy Tenney/GodChasers.network
P.O. Box 3355, Pineville, Louisiana 71361-3355
318.44CHASE (318.442.4273)